THE NEW ZEN GARDEN

THE NEW ZEN GARDEN

DESIGNING QUIET SPACES

JOSEPH CALI

WITH PHOTOGRAPHS BY
SATOSHI ASAKAWA

KODANSHA INTERNATIONAL
Tokyo • New York • London

CONTENTS

INTRODUCTION 6

CHAPTER 1 THE ROOTS OF THE JAPANESE GARDEN 8

Zen and Its Influence 9
The Evolution of the Japanese Garden 12
Garden Types 20
  Stone-and-Sand Gardens 20
  Scenic and Stroll Gardens 20
  Tea Gardens 21
  Courtyard Gardens 21

CHAPTER 2 LAYOUT AND ENCLOSURE 22

A Small Courtyard Garden 23
  Site Conditions 24
  Needs and Desires 24
  General Principles of Garden Design 24
  A Plan for a Courtyard Garden 25

A Large Stroll Garden 26
  Site Conditions 26
  Needs and Desires 27
  General Principles of Garden Design 28
  Basic Plan for a Large Stroll Garden 28

A Medium-size Stone-and-Sand Garden 29
  Site Conditions 29
  Needs and Desires 30
  General Principles of Garden Design 30

Practice 33
  Enclosures 33

BUILDING A TRADITIONAL CLAY WALL IN THE *NURU* STYLE 36
by Yasumoro Sadao

CHAPTER 3 STONE-AND-SAND GARDENS 38

Stone Basics 42
Stone Groupings 44
Placing and Grouping Stones 45
Additional Uses of Stone 48
Types of Stone 50
  Granite · Blue Stone · Volcanic Rock · Marble · Volcanic Tuff ·
  Slate · Pumice · Cobblestones · Pebbles · Sand and Gravel

Laying Gravel and Sand and Designing Patterns 54
  Rakes 54

ARRANGING A "DRY WATERFALL" 58
by Masuno Shunmyo

CHAPTER 4 WATER AND RELATED GARDEN FIXTURES 60

Pond Design 61

Pond Construction 63

Streams 64

Waterfalls 66

Producing Sound with Water 67

Stone Waterbasins 68

Stone Lanterns 70
 Kasuga Lantern · *Oribe* Lantern · *Yukimi* Lantern · Valley Lantern · Signpost Lantern · *Okidoro* Lantern · Sleeve Lantern

Lighting 72
 Utilitarian Lighting
 Dramatic Lighting

LIGHTING IN A SMALL VERANDA GARDEN 74
by Yagi Kenichi

CHAPTER 5 PLANTINGS AND OTHER GARDEN FEATURES 76

Preferred Plantings 78
 The Color Palette and Traditional Plantings 78
 Other Trees and Shrubs 78
 Grasses and Moss 79

Pruning and Shaping 81

Stepping Stones and Walkways 82

BUILDING A WALKWAY IN THE SEMIFORMAL STYLE 84
by Oguchi Motomi

LIST OF PLANTS 86
 Evergreen Trees · Evergreen Shrubs · Deciduous Trees · Deciduous Shrubs · Herbaceous Plants, Perennials, Ground Covers, etc.

BIBLIOGRAPHY 88
ACKNOWLEDGMENTS 88

NOTE: Japanese personal names appear in the traditional order, surname preceding given name.

Published by Kodansha International Ltd., 17–14 Otowa 1-chome, Bunkyo-ku, Tokyo 112–8652, and Kodansha America, Inc.

Distributed in the United States by Kodansha America, Inc., and in the United Kingdom and continental Europe by Kodansha Europe Ltd.

Copyright © 2004 by Joseph Cali. All rights reserved. Printed in Japan.

First edition, 2004

10 9 8 7 6 5 4 3 2 1   09 08 07 06 05 04
ISBN 4–7700–2981–0

INTRODUCTION

This book is about creating a comfortable and peaceful space known as a Japanese garden, and about how such gardens have evolved under the influence of Zen Buddhism. The particular examples we have chosen to focus on are by and large modern gardens, created by designers and gardeners of various backgrounds and specialties. For the most part they are small-scale, house gardens, and many of them are dry gardens employing stone and sand as their chief medium of expression.

Gardens today are undergoing great changes that reflect general trends in society. On the whole, gardens are becoming very simple, not only for philosophical or design reasons but also due to economic and social conditions, such as smaller and more mobile families. Desire for lower costs and easy maintenance, as well as multiple use and nonconventional spaces, all play a factor. However, the tenets of garden-making in Japan have remained basically unchanged for a thousand years. Many of these tenets were originally imported from China and modified over time to suit the needs of the Japanese environment and temperament.

Another import that has had an enormous effect on garden-making—and every other aspect of life in Japan—is Buddhism. This religion, which started from one man's search for the meaning of life, spread from India to China, and from there to the Japanese archipelago. After Buddhism took root in Japan, various sects or schools of thought developed. One such sect that began to flourish around the thirteenth century is Zen.

Today, opinions about what constitutes a Zen-influenced garden vary widely. Some assert no such influence exists, while others confidently attribute gardens to Zen concepts without knowing who actually designed and built the gardens in question or what the designers intended.

The lack of specifics that distinguishes Zen perhaps makes such a debate inevitable. In ancient times Zen was described by Huike, the second patriarch of Zen, thus:

A special transmission outside the scriptures,
No dependence on the written word,
Direct pointing at the soul of man,
Seeing one's own nature and attaining Buddhahood.

Given such an enigmatic description, it is no wonder that different interpretations of the doctrine proliferate. Its very nature consigns rules, symbols, and definitions to those who are still "seeking" and have not yet found the "answer" known as Enlightenment.

This book takes no stand in that debate, nor advances any

new theories, preferring instead to enjoy and admire the diversity of design and approach in the firm belief that the goal is the same. That goal is the innocent joy of creation and the conscious effort to foster what is best in the human spirit through making and maintaining a garden.

This book adopts the point of view that the real "way" of Zen or any other religion or philosophy is based on practice, in this case, pertaining to the garden. Garden-making is an art, and, as with any art, certain forms and ways of seeing result from the way the art is practiced. For example, some shapes achieved by sculpting in soft clay would not result from sculpting a piece of stone, regardless of philosophy. More importantly, the character of the person who chooses self-expression in soft, malleable clay may be fundamentally different from someone who prefers to hammer at stone that resists being changed.

In the arts of painting and sculpture, Zen artists chose to make realistic images of their teachers rather than elaborate images showing Buddhas in their glorious heavens. They also preferred objects found in nature and depicted them in black and white. When it came to gardens, these were reduced to the most enduring elements of stone and sand.

Many of the gardens in this book reflect the abstract thought and reduction to essentials indicative of Zen. Sometimes this is readily apparent; at others it is not. Sometimes it results from a consciousness on the part of the creator; at others it results from the cultural environment to which Zen belongs. In either case, the resultant features and forms are representative of modern Japanese gardens and of the culture that produced them.

In order to understand the culture reflected in the unique character of these gardens, this book begins with a brief history of Japanese gardens and a list of garden types. After that we discuss designing and building a garden, using both traditional and nontraditional techniques. The captions to the photographs and illustrations supplement the text and provide a link between traditional techniques and the modern gardens that have evolved from them.

In conclusion, I hope this book will appeal to anyone interested in Japanese arts in general or, more specifically, in understanding or creating a Zen-style garden of their own. As those of us raised in different cultures seek to learn a new visual language, the principles and practices outlined here will undoubtedly undergo further changes in backyards outside Japan, influenced by other cultures and experiences. This is as it should be.

CHAPTER 1

THE ROOTS OF THE JAPANESE GARDEN

ZEN AND ITS INFLUENCE

Early to pre-modern Japanese civilization was shaped in part by Chinese culture through direct contact or as filtered through the Korean Peninsula. Garden design arrived in Japan between the sixth and seventh centuries A.D., in the first great wave of cultural influences from China that affected the arts, government, architecture, city planning, and the written language.

Buddhism was slower to arrive. After the Enlightenment of the Indian nobleman Siddhartha Gautama (ca. 563–483 B.C.), Buddhism spread to China during the Han dynasty (206 B.C.–A.D. 220) and flourished during the Six Dynasties (A.D. 220–589), subsequently becoming one of the main Asian religions. It entered Japan around A.D. 552, when the king of Paekche (part of present-day Korea) sent Buddhist images and sutras to the Yamato court. In the early seventh century, Buddhism became a point of contention between the Soga clan, who wanted it accepted as the official religion, and the Mononobe and Nakatomi clans, who saw it as a threat to the native Shinto religion (and their own power base). A pivotal struggle lead to the demise of the Mononobe and with it the official acceptance and subsequent spread of Buddhism in Japan.

The roots of Japanese Zen can be traced to the Chan sect of Chinese Buddhism ("zen" is the Japanese reading of "chan"), which came to Japan in the second great wave of Chinese influence in the thirteenth and fourteenth centuries. Chan, as it was practiced in Japan, was highly ascetic and appealed to the newly powerful warrior class of the Kamakura period (1185–1333). Its emphasis on self-reliance rather than salvation, and sincerity rather than status, gave it a wider appeal than the esoteric aspects of Buddhism favored by the aristocrats of the Heian court (794–1185). Aesthetically and philosophically, it has been influential in shaping Japanese art and culture ever since. First, however, Chan Buddhism, formed by the influence of Chinese

A nineteenth-century visualization of *shinden*-style architecture showing the *shinden* main building in the center and annexes connected by covered corridors. The entrance on the right leads to a flat, spacious area covered with white gravel, flanked by a pond to the south and connected to an island by a Chinese-style bridge. A fishing pavilion extends out over the pond at the lower left.

The much-photographed dry sand garden of the Miyako Hotel in Kyoto adds a mood of profound silence more indicative of a mountain monastery than a hotel. The deep eaves and hanging bamboo screens exaggerate the horizontal view of the scene, in the same manner that gardens have been viewed since the eighth century.

Taoist thought on the original Indian belief system, was to be shaped one last time into Zen by the indigenous beliefs of the Japanese people.

The native animistic beliefs of the Japanese known as Shinto ("Way of the Gods") are not unlike the beliefs of early man in all parts of the world. These myths and beliefs were first recorded in written works of the eighth century, but the roots of Japanese civilization are believed to date from the Jomon period, beginning about 10,000 B.C. Unfathomable natural forces, including life and death, which are given concrete form and revered as gods, lie at the very heart of all human mythology and religion. It is the particular way in which human consciousness of "the self" is interwoven with this awe and reverence for nature that gives a particular character to a religion or culture. Of special interest in this respect are man's feelings of integration in or isolation from nature. Whereas the Judeo–Christian world-view isolates God outside the world of man, the Shinto and Buddhist views do not. In particular, the self-view of the Japanese can be said historically to be one in which nature is primary and man achieves his highest level when he is fully integrated with nature, rather than when nature is shaped by him. As the mythologist Joseph Campbell has stated, "The basic moral idea [of Shinto] is that the process of nature cannot be evil . . . [and] that the pure heart follows the processes of nature." In the desire to realize human integration with a cosmic natural order, Zen and Shinto have one and the same goal.

Ultimately, a desire for harmony and the accommodation of conflicting interests resulted in Buddhist temples initially being built on the grounds of Shinto shrines, once "permission" of the god inhabiting that shrine had been requested and received. Prince Shotoku (574–622), who was instrumental in the development of Buddhism and was one of its greatest early champions, issued a decree around 607, which formally established the native religion (Shinto) as the core set of beliefs and rituals of the imperial house. This formal recognition helped smooth the way for the propagation of Buddhism by allowing supporters of the native gods to respect the emperor's leadership without feeling supplanted or debased. From about the tenth century, a theory known as *honji suijaku* ("original prototype, local manifestation") was advanced. This held that *kami*, as Shinto divinities are known, were local manifestations of Buddhist deities and that worship of *kami* was equal to worship of Buddhist deities in the form of *kami*. In Japan, certain stones, trees, mountains, waterfalls, and other natural features were revered as places where *kami* resided and

A detail of the dry sand-and-stone garden (*kare san-sui*) at Ryoanji in Kyoto. The most renown of all the Zen-inspired gardens of stone and sand has become, for better or worse, a powerful symbol of Zen philosophy and Japanese culture in general.

shrines were often no more than simple gravel-covered clearings around a stone draped with *shimenawa* (cords of twisted rice straw) or *gohei* (zigzag paper streamers) to mark it as a god-seat. Buddhism ushered in a new culture of temple-building and related arts and crafts.

In a similar way, cultural and technical influences, first from China and Korea and later from Europe and America, were absorbed and modified by native beliefs and sensitivities. Synthesis and coexistence of otherwise irreconcilable forces (*shugo*) is the modus operandi of Japanese society. Joseph Campbell referred to theologist Rudolf Otto's concept of the numinous—a sense of wonder and openness to spiritual experience—to describe pre-Buddhist Japan. The seeds of Zen fell onto this fertile ground.

As Asian scholar-curator Langdon Warner pointed out in *The Enduring Art of Japan*, Shinto belief in *kami* penetrated every aspect of daily life. Particularly in the life of the craftsman, Shinto ritual was integral to the organized preservation of the myths, traditions, and secrets of the trades. In a fundamental way, failing to worship the *kami*, or failing to follow the rules of one's trade, were grievous sins. Thus, the only correct way to build a house, plant rice, distill liquor, or forge a sword, was also the religious way. The attitude of reverence toward the gods and toward one's own work were inseparable and formed the basic morality of the society. This attitude found a welcome parallel in the non-judgemental Zen attitude that "all things are Buddha things."

THE EVOLUTION OF THE JAPANESE GARDEN

Though Buddhism was introduced to Japan around 552, it was not until the early seventh century that both Buddhism and Chinese culture began to exert a strong influence on Japanese culture and on the garden. However, when we speak of the first Japanese gardens, we are generally speaking of gardens from around the Heian period.

At that time gardens were associated either with residences of the aristocracy or with select Buddhist temples. Aristocratic gardens were chiefly playgrounds that adopted literary as well as natural landscape themes. They were places to write poetry and engage in other forms of group performance and entertainment, and were often viewed from small boats floating on a pond as well as from pavilions extending over the pond itself. Such occasions were described in the eleventh-century novel *The Tale of Genji*.

Though aristocratic gardens from this era no longer exist, descriptions such as those in the eleventh-century *Sakuteiki* (Notes on Garden Design) give a clear indication of what they were like. These gardens were built on the south side of a *shinden*-style building, which was made up of a series of large and small wooden pavilions raised on low stilts and connected by exterior, covered corridors. The dictates of geomancy called for a pond to the south of the building fed by a stream that flowed under the building from the northeast. A large expanse of white gravel between the building and the pond offered space for guests to gather. The pond was laid out with one, two, or three islands connected by arched bridges in the red-painted, Chinese manner. Stone, mounds of earth, and plantings were placed to give the impression of the shore of an ocean, a marsh pond, or another body of water. These gardens with artificial hills and ponds are known as *tsukiyama*-style gardens.

Temple gardens were generally laid out on an east–west axis, responding to the belief in the Western Paradise of Amida Buddha. The Shingon, Tendai, and Jodo ("Pure Land") sects of Buddhism, which taught

More an echo of a garden than a garden itself, this *tsubo niwa* by architect Nagata Masahito is more about isolating a certain space within the house as something other than interior space, and fulfilling one of the *tsubo niwa*'s original functions of bringing fresh air and natural light into a room.

A sensitivity to changing light and a delicate richness of forms and textures is a hallmark of Japanese aesthetics as revealed in places such as Katsura Villa and this *washi*-covered room in a small apartment house by architect Kawaguchi Michimasa. The crossed stalks of bamboo, looking much like a hanging-scroll painting, are planted in one of the many courtyard gardens (*tsubo niwa*) that dot the complex.

that the believer would be transported to the Western Paradise if he or she sought salvation from the Buddha, appealed to the aristocracy who sponsored these temples. This influence led to the development of gardens representing paradise. Such gardens consisted of a large pond in front of the main building, with a single island and bridges from the near and far shore, connected in such a way that they formed a central "avenue" leading to the main entrance of the temple. Ponds were filled with lotus blossoms, symbolizing Enlightenment. Common stone arrangements, such as *sanzon seki* (a three-stone arrangement based on the conventional depiction of the Buddha flanked by two bodhisattvas), which first appeared in the sixth century, developed fully in the Heian period.

Violent disturbances from the late eleventh to the early twelfth centuries resulted in the fall of the old Heian aristocracy. The feudal age that followed, beginning with the shift of power to Kamakura, south of Tokyo, embraced the "Way of the Warrior" and the cult of the shogun (a position appointed by the emperor and roughly equivalent to "military dictator"). Many new social structures and forms of culture were introduced in this period, the most influential and most enduring of which was Zen.

In 1338, the Ashikaga clan rose to power and moved the government back to Kyoto, though not into the control of the emperor. Their base was the Muromachi district of Kyoto that lends its name to the age. It is here, in this caldron-mix of warrior and indulgent court life, that art and culture flourished as never before. It is here that the Noh theater developed as an expression of the beauty of nothingness; here that the tea ceremony began to flourish and leave its indelible mark; here, too, that the implacable search for the "way" culminated in the Zen stone-and-sand gardens as embodied in Ryoanji and Daitokuji (both in Kyoto) and many other now-famous temple gardens of the fourteenth and fifteenth centuries. Many critics consider this period, with its symbolic and abstract gardens, to represent the peak of Japanese garden design.

A second wave of Chinese trade and influence took place between the thirteenth and sixteenth centuries. Gardens of this period are marked by new visual ideas based on Southern Song–dynasty (1128–1279) landscape painting, and an influx of Chan teacher-monks from China such as Lanxi Daolong (1213–78), and Yishan Yining (1247–1317), a priest-emissary of Kublai Khan. Yining was a teacher of the Zen priest Muso Soseki (1275–1351), one of the most influential people in terms of the spread of Zen and the design of gardens in the Kamakura period. Another important Zen priest, Ikkyu Sojun (1394–1481), became the abbot of Daitokuji temple at a time when the city of Sakai was at the center of the China trade and its leading citizens were defining the art of tea (*chado*). Along with the poet Socho (1448–1532), Ikkyu's emphasis on sincerity and his popularization of the idea of a mountain hut retreat within an urban setting greatly inspired the masters of the tea ceremony. The idea and design of the "dewy path" (*roji*), as the tea garden is known, evolved during this era, as did the idea of the tea gathering as a spiritual exercise closely related to Zen meditation. Emphasis was placed on developing true taste (*suki*) through simplicity and sincerity. Creativity

With examples of actual *shinden*-style architecture no longer extant, much speculation takes place about what they were like. This pavilion in the "geese in flight" (*gankokei*) zigzag form developed in the Heian period is housed under a glass roof (not shown) at Meguro Gajoen in Tokyo. This view shows what would have been a north garden close to the building and containing the "source" of the water that would have served to feed the pond on the southern side.

and seeing things in a new light (*mitate*) is part of this, and reveals itself in the garden in such aspects as the novel use of recycled stones and other materials for waterbasins (*tsukubai*) and stone lanterns (*ishidoro*).

Another important development in this era was the rise of professional gardeners. Many came from the lowest ranks of society, the so-called river people (*kawaramono*). Current scholarship generally accepts that a considerable number of the gardens of the era were attributed to famous people on the basis of either their status or their general influence on garden art and theory, and acknowledges the contributions of the often nameless men who actually chose the materials, laid out the gardens, and supervised the placement of materials. The garden-building priests (*ishitate-so*) who carried much of the burden of creating gardens in earlier periods gradually handed over the work to those such as Zen'ami (1386–1482), a *kawaramono* who gained the recognition of the shogun Ashikaga Yoshimasa for his excellent skill in garden craft. Many men of less than aristocratic birth, who attained a high measure of professional skill during this period, became indispensable to a new class of leaders that needed advice and assistance in matters of culture.

The Momoyama period (1568–1600) that followed was in most respects a continuation of the Muromachi period (1333–1568). The Ashikagas were succeeded by Oda Nobunaga (1534–82) and then by Toyotomi Hideyoshi (1537–98). Both men continued to wage war and managed more or less to unify the country. Many castles and gardens were built, especially under Hideyoshi, and this may also be a clue as to why some feel that garden design declined after the Muromachi period. With the rise of ever more autocratic and powerful leaders, gardens were created less for priests and the educated elite and more to fulfill the demands and prerogatives of the warrior seeking the status of a lord. This can be seen in the excesses of Hideyoshi's Sanbo-in, a leading example of gardens of the period. Though the garden is skillfully made, the designer was forced to employ hundreds of colorful stones that Hideyoshi had accumulated.

In the next era, the trend of gardens created by professionals for the purpose of entertainment on a grand scale continued, resulting in another distinctive Japanese garden style. Around 1603, Tokugawa Ieyasu (1543–1616) seized the reins of power from Hideyoshi's son and moved the capital to the eastern village of Edo (present-day Tokyo). Ieyasu was able both to finish unifying the country and to bring about an era of stability and relative prosperity that lasted more than two hundred and fifty years, known today as the Edo period (1600–1868). New power alignments and new wealth meant new buildings and larger estates. The daimyo "stroll" or "many-pleasure" garden (*kaiyu-shiki teien*) was distinct from previous upper-class gardens in that it was laid out with a large central pond encircled by paths, incorporated many different garden styles, and was built for neither a temple nor a residence but solely for the purpose of entertainment. The stability of the Tokugawa regime, the new availability of materials and resources, the desire for travel (in a country where overseas travel was banned), and an urge to relive the greatness of the past, influenced the creation of the Japanese stroll garden.

The refuse hole (*chiriana*) shown here is a small but important feature of most tea gardens. Before guests arrive the garden is cleaned and several freshly cut branches along with the bamboo chopsticks used to pick up such small refuse as fallen leaves are placed in the *chiriana* to symbolize the spiritual cleansing process each person who enters the garden will undergo.

Three of the greatest gardens of the early Edo period were neither created by the shoguns nor located in Tokyo. The garden of the Katsura Villa (1620–45), attributed to Prince Toshihito (1579–1629) and his son Toshitada (1619–62), was one of these. This garden, like many of the period, was a major feature of the retirement retreat of an imperial family. Various pavilions and modest-sized guesthouses, as well as numerous teahouses scattered over vast holdings, make up this retreat landscaped in a variety of styles. As such, it is considered a prototype of the stroll garden and a model for many that followed. The Heian period, as epitomized in *The Tale of Genji*, still formed the basis of an ideal world for which the nobility, marginalized by the warrior class, still longed. It is said of Prince Toshihito that "the garden with literary beauty was what he desired."

Two other magnificent stroll gardens of the period can be found on the grounds of the Sento Gosho (1634) and the twenty-three-acre Shugakuin Villa (1659), built for Emperor Go-Mizunoo (1596–1680; r. 1611–29). A noteworthy characteristic of these stroll gardens is the sophisticated use of the technique known as "borrowed scenery" (*shakkei*), in which areas of the garden are constructed in such a way as to incorporate the landscape outside the garden, including surrounding views or vistas. Another technique developed in earlier times and known as "hide and reveal" (*miekakure*) is exploited to the fullest in the stroll garden. Unlike gardens with fixed views meant to be seen from inside a building, stroll gardens require the viewer to move through the grounds and "discover" sights and views that unfold from certain positions along fixed pathways. Indeed, stroll gardens borrowed from almost every garden type up to this period, making extensive use of large and small stepping stones and stone lanterns (originally developed in teahouse gardens), ponds, islands, artificial hills, and the representation of famous views from China and Japan. However, these gardens, like their predecessors, remained the exclusive retreats of the most powerful and wealthy.

The "paradise garden" of Jodo Buddhism underwent changes that developed in parallel to the stroll garden of the daimyo. The stability of the Edo period brought with it a newly prosperous urban class that had money and broader interests but limited rights to acquire land or build pleasure gardens. One outlet for the more erudite of this class was the culture of tea, with its setting of "an urban hut" in a garden or the small courtyard gardens, known as *tsubo niwa*, integrated into the structure of the Kyoto-style townhouse. For the less privileged, religious pilgrimages gained popularity at this time, and the practice of touring a series of temples became a frequent pastime for commoners of all ranks and exposed the populace to a large number of new gardens. Some massive pilgrimages, called *okage mairi* ("thanksgiving pilgrimages"), saw millions of people clogging the roads for months at a time. The same techniques of "hide and reveal" and "borrowed scenery" used in stroll gardens were employed in these temple compounds as well. Flower-viewing became linked to spiritual devotion in the pleasure gardens of the common people.

One outstanding designer of the era was Kobori Enshu (1579–1647), who was an aristocrat and a commissioner of public works. As the latter, he designed and oversaw the building of a number of castles and temples. As a member of the Kyoto elite and prominent student of Furuta Oribe—the successor to the illustrious tea master Sen no Rikyu and the most influential tea master of his time—he was both educated and cultivated. As a high officer of the shogunal regime, he had at his disposal vast resources at a time when schematic drawing, mathematics, and the distribution of labor were playing an important role in rationalizing design and construction. Enshu's designs make full use of borrowed scenery in the same spirit of creativity that motivated other tea masters of his time. He is a master of thematic allusion and the grand scale. In many ways Enshu was the first and most influential landscape architect in Japan.

The antithesis of a classic garden, the focus here has been abstracted to a dialog between surface and light, exactly what you might expect for the home of a photographer. Paving stone and cobbles add their comment to the ongoing discussion of interior versus exterior space in this garden by Kawaguchi Michimasa.

By the early eighteenth century, all garden design styles and conventions had stabilized. There remained only the import of new influences and the reinterpretation of old ones.

The Meiji (1868–1912) and Taisho (1912–26) eras mark the beginning of the period when Western culture was imported wholesale and influenced every aspect of Japanese life (much as Chinese culture had centuries earlier). After several hundred years of strict isolation, Japan began a Western-style modernization that altered the face of the country forever. One aspect of this modernization that affected garden design was the introduction of Western-style buildings and gardens, particularly those of Victorian England. With this influx, the need to define "Japanese" as a garden type (as opposed to Western) resulted in a large number of books on the subject, as well as newly founded educational institutions and groups of professionals such as the Japan Garden Association (1918) and the Japanese Institute of Landscape Architecture (1925). This was a period of research, reevaluation, and the quest for definition of garden styles, which were subsequently classified as *tsukiyama* (artificial hill and pond), *hira niwa* (flat garden), and *cha niwa* (tea garden), in three degrees of formality, *shin*, *gyo*, and *so* (formal, semiformal, and informal).

The Showa (1926–89) and Heisei (1989–) eras are notable for changes in the nature of spaces provided for gardens, as well as the increased use of processed materials and exotic plantings. Space allocation for home gardens is still common but sizes are minimal. New garden spaces—such as roofs, verandas, hotel entrances, office building lobbies, and shopping complexes—are being utilized, and various combinations of traditional and modern techniques employed. The stone-and-sand garden (*kare sansui*) experienced new-found domestic and international attention due in large measure to the efforts of garden designer Shigemori Mirei (1896–1975) and the "discovery" of the stone-and-sand garden's affinity for modern architecture. The writings of novelist Shiga Naoya (1883–1971) and activities of garden designer Tono Takuma (1891–1985) also contributed to the recognition of the stone-and-sand garden as a singular garden type. Simultaneously, the writings of Buddhist philosopher Suzuki Daisetz (1870–1966), philosopher Hisamatsu Shin'ichi (1889–1980), and author Loraine Kuck, an authority on Japanese gardens, contributed to the linking of stone-and-sand gardens to Zen philosophy.

Today, gardens are created primarily by *niwashi* (garden designer/builders), *uekiya* (gardeners who are mostly involved in growing trees and the maintenance of gardens), landscape architects, architects, Buddhist monks, and, of course, laymen.

The tendency now is to separate classic-style gardens from modern gardens. Classic gardens are viewed as those that adhere to design principles espoused since the Heian era and incorporates classic elements such as sleeve fences, stone waterbasins, and stone lanterns. Such classic gardens have become almost exclusively associated with *niwashi* trained in the traditional master–apprentice system. Much of their work is focused on small-scale, private gardens and the restoration or remaking of older gardens. It is essentially a craftsman's profession, and most *niwashi* are physically involved with garden construction, though many are not skilled as draftsman.

Modern gardens have become associated with architects, who may or may not have formal training in garden design, and landscape architects, who graduate from a university-accredited program and are primarily engaged in large-scale public or commercial projects, often in association with general contractors, city governments, and architects. Modern gardens may—or, more often, may not—include classic elements, or include them in a highly abstracted form. While classic design principles are usually observed, these too are often abstracted and distilled to a minimum.

GARDEN TYPES

STONE-AND-SAND GARDENS—*KARE SANSUI*

The main focus of this book is the *kare sansui*, which is most closely associated with the influence of Zen and Zen's practitioners. Although this type of dry landscape garden predates Zen, the majority of examples can be traced to the influence of Zen from the thirteenth century on. These gardens generally include some plant life, especially moss. However, the dominant feature of the gardens that began to appear in Zen Buddhist temples of the fifteenth century is the abstractness of the vast areas of raked gravel representing water, and the placement of large and small stones in some sort of thematic arrangement. These gardens are almost always viewed from the vantage point of an adjacent building and are usually laid out within a limited, geometric space. They are almost always flat gardens, surrounded with a wall that isolates them and forms a backdrop.

SCENIC AND STROLL GARDENS —*TSUKIYAMA* AND *KAIYU-SHIKI TEIEN*

The *tsukiyama*, in which artificial hills, ponds, islands, and waterfalls are created, and the *kaiyu-shiki teien* ("many-pleasure garden," or "stroll garden"), common during the Edo period, represent the majority of large-scale Japanese gardens, many of which have become public parks. The *tsukiyama* garden is usually—but not always—viewed from inside a building. In the broadest terms, it is any type of garden that attempts to create a single, natural-looking scene comprising hills, water, plantings, and stone. In contrast, the stroll garden combines a series of different scenes visually isolated from, but physically connected to, each other. The stroll garden is viewed by walking along predetermined paths and circling a large pond to discover interesting sights and scenes. In both types, famous places that are either real or literary are represented or referred to in such a way as to be recognizable to viewers.

TEA GARDENS—*CHA NIWA* OR *ROJI*

The tea garden is an essential setting for the teahouse in which the tea ceremony is performed. It was developed to enhance the experience of the ceremony, both as an inspirational setting (perhaps reminiscent of some small mountain hermitage) and as a device for the symbolic passage from the "profane" world outside the garden gate to the "sacred" world inside the teahouse. Characteristics of this garden include the division between outer and inner gardens through the use of a gate. The gardens contain a waiting-bench (*koshikake machiai*), waterbasin (*tsukubai*), and stone lantern (*ishidoro*). Stepping stones (*tobi ishi*) are placed to lead the guest from one area to the next, and the whole atmosphere is contrived to be simple but highly symbolic and planned with the utmost care.

COURTYARD GARDENS—*TSUBO NIWA*

The courtyard garden has no strict definition of its appearance other than its small size. It takes its name from the Japanese term *tsubo*, a measurement equal to 36 square feet (3.3 square meters) and meant as a figurative reference to the garden's small size. The modern roots of the *tsubo niwa* date from the fifteenth-century architectural style of Kyoto merchant townhouses, which were defined by long, narrow lots punctuated by larger and smaller courtyards intended to ventilate and bring light into the deeper recesses of the building. Courtyard spaces were also ideal for the creation of the intimate gardens that evolved into the modern *tsubo niwa*, such as the one depicted here by architect Nagano Kazuo. These most often incorporate elements from the tea garden such as the waterbasin and stone lantern, along with some shade-tolerant plantings. Such spaces are commonly found in courtyards of private dwellings, or—increasingly in metropolitan areas—on back porches, verandas, rooftops, entranceways, office building lobbies, and restaurants. One aspect of the *tsubo niwa* is the sense of a microcosm of nature and a close look at changes of the seasons. Although not, strictly speaking, a separate type of garden, it is often spoken of as such.

CHAPTER 2

LAYOUT AND ENCLOSURE

Intimacy and sensitivity are subtly expressed in this backyard *tsubo niwa* by garden designer Ogino Toshiya. The slender tree has been replanted among an arrangement of mounded earth and "falling rocks" at an angle reflecting the way it originally grew from the side of a cliff. The whiteness of the wall constructed behind it seems to emphasize the fragile and delicate balance of nature of which we are all a part.

The layout and the arrangement of stones are regarded as the most important aspects of the Japanese garden. In this section we will look at some design principles and sample layouts, as well as the closely related issue of enclosing the garden with one or more walls and fences common to the Japanese garden. The use of stone will be covered in the next chapter.

In terms of the overall design, the physical characteristics of the space available for the garden—that is, the size, shape, and other important factors specific to the site—should be considered first. The second consideration will be your needs and desires. Finally, the correct design solution will involve applying the aspects of the Japanese garden that best satisfy your needs while meeting all of the site conditions.

To gain a better understanding of how to go about the layout, let's look at three examples of varying size.

A SMALL COURTYARD GARDEN—*TSUBO NIWA*

The first example is a small courtyard garden suitable for an apartment veranda, a townhouse patio, or a corner of a larger yard space. The increasing prevalence of high-rise apartment buildings, and smaller living quarters in general, has created new applications for the *tsubo niwa* as a veranda or patio garden. This type of garden has a long history in Japan. It began as a courtyard garden between pavilions connected by long, open corridors in the *shinden*-style architecture of the eighth to fourteenth centuries, and later evolved into small semi-interior gardens in traditional long, narrow Kyoto homes of the sixteenth century known as *machiya*.

A classic courtyard garden in a modern context, rendered here by architect Nagasaka Dai. The bamboo enclosure tempers the light and provides privacy without inhibiting the flow of air, while enhancing a feeling of intimacy with nature.

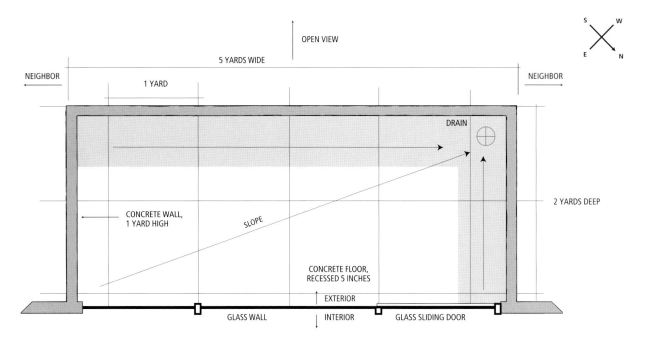

PLAN DRAWING OF VERANDA.

SITE CONDITIONS

Our example is based on an apartment veranda as viewed from inside the apartment. Many different designs are possible within the limitations of a small space and the other conditions imposed by the site in our example (such as not being able to affix anything permanently). The physical conditions and how they potentially relate to the final design are listed first:

- The size is 5 yards wide by 2 yards deep (4.5 by 1.8 m), and strictly rectangular in shape. In terms of the design this means that relatively small plantings and fixtures will be needed.
- The veranda is surrounded by a painted concrete wall 1 yard high and 6 inches thick (90 by 15 cm) on three sides. The fourth side is the floor-to-ceiling glass wall of the apartment, with a sliding glass door on the right side. For the design this means several things. First, the veranda is very boxy, with a lot of straight lines that will probably need to be softened. Second, the location indicates that however the garden is used, it will primarily be viewed from inside the adjacent room.
- The veranda floor is concrete with a gentle slope toward the right rear corner, where there is a drain. The floor of the veranda is lower than the interior floor, which means there is a small step down from inside the apartment. Any planting on the veranda will need to be in planters, and a removable surfacing material to cover the concrete, without clogging the drain, will need to be used.

NEEDS AND DESIRES

These are the main physical characteristics and their implications for the design. Next come your needs: what do you want from the garden? Everyone's response to this question will, of course, be different. Here is one possible list:

- Some additional privacy in relation to the neighbor's veranda.
- The ability to enjoy a view of the garden from inside the apartment, plus the ability to enter and enjoy the garden, including a space for a small table and at least two chairs.
- A quiet, shady atmosphere that reduces some of the glare of the setting sun in the apartment without relying on curtains.

GENERAL PRINCIPLES OF GARDEN DESIGN

Now that we have the site conditions and our wish list, let's look at some general principles of Japanese garden design. These will apply whatever the size or intended use of the garden. The Japanese garden favors:

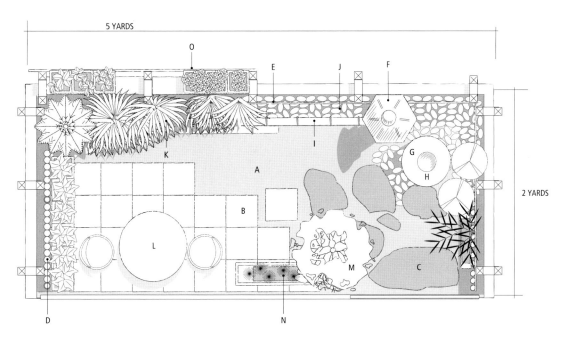

5 YARDS

2 YARDS

LAYOUT OF VERANDA GARDEN.

A. Bed of rough sand, 1/8 to 3/16 (2 to 3 mm) diameter, about 2 inches (5 cm) deep. B. Square, unpolished paving stone. C. Rough paving stone, about 2 1/2 inches (6 cm) thick. D. Bamboo poles. E. Wood plank and bamboo wall. F. Stone lantern. G. Stone or ceramic waterbasin. H. Stone for pedestal of basin. I. Half-split bamboo, 3 to 4 inches (8 to 10 cm) in diameter, used as a retainer for sand. J. Small cobblestone or large pebbles. K. Various potted plantings. L. Table and chairs M. Dwarf maple. N. Group of bonsai. O. Additional shelves and plantings.

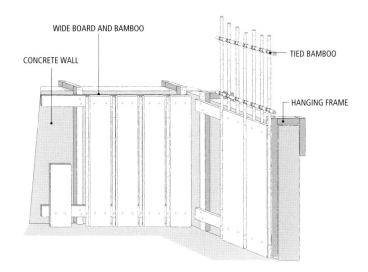

VERANDA GARDEN, PERSPECTIVE VIEW.

- An asymmetrical layout, and organic shapes over geometric ones
- Naturalistic groupings of rocks, water, and/or plantings
- Irregular edges over clean, sharp edges
- Unpolished stone over polished stone
- Trees, bushes, moss, and leafy plants over large areas of flowers
- Thoughtful reflection on the activity of nature in all seasons
- An atmosphere of calm and repose

A PLAN FOR A COURTYARD GARDEN

With these three lists in mind, let's look at one possible layout. The design uses alternating rough wooden planks and cut bamboo poles on a frame of wood strips to conceal the concrete walls and form tall partitions on the right and left sides. These side partitions use wooden planks only up to the height of the concrete wall. The bamboo poles extend to the full height of about 1.8 yards (162 cm). Shorter poles are inserted into the gap between the longer ones and tied to horizontal poles for support. This creates an open trellis through which wind can blow unobstructed.

A frame of wood stripping is hung from the concrete to support the planking. A long narrow planter about 8 inches (20 cm) deep is set at the base of the wall on the right side to hold bamboo, which will grow tall and fill the open spaces between the cut bamboo poles. The narrow stalks can be tied to the poles for support if necessary and are easily cut back if they become too tall. The left side is planted with dwarf cypress or spruce and some other leafy evergreen plant with seasonal flowering such as azalea or osmanthus.

Flagstones and unpolished, square-cut paving stones are placed, then the joints are filled with course sand or fine gravel. Half-cut bamboo of about 3 inches (8 cm) in diameter is used as a frame to contain the sand. A fine stainless steel mesh is placed over the drain, and the back right corner and space along the back wall are

WIDE BOARD AND BAMBOO

CONCRETE WALL

TIED BAMBOO

HANGING FRAME

DETAIL OF HANGING-FRAME CONSTRUCTION.

This jewel-like veranda garden by Kyoto architect Yokouchi Toshihito is a true urban retreat. Neither the practical addition of a bamboo bench nor the houses of neighbors viewed through the hanging bamboo screens seems out of synch with the harmony of this space.

filled with large black or blue-gray pebbles. The mesh will need to be cleaned periodically.

Near the right corner a "foundation stone" (*garan seki*) is placed and leveled, and a stone or a lighter-weight ceramic waterbasin is set on top of it. Next to this a stone lantern (check the maximum weight allowable on the veranda with your building supervisor) is assembled and made level. Candles or a small oil lamp will be used in the lantern to provide atmospheric light. Additional shade-tolerant, leafy plantings will be placed around the base of other plantings, along the wall, and on small shelves attached to the plank fencing. A prized bonsai rests close to the glass, next to a potted dwarf Japanese maple in an unglazed planter. The maple will blaze red and drop its leaves in autumn. Finally, the table and chairs are set up, and all is ready for a perfect tea-drinking, sunset-watching, Japanese-style veranda. This design is related to the classic Kyoto-style courtyard garden of the sixteenth and seventeenth centuries.

A LARGE STROLL GARDEN—*KAIYU-SHIKI TEIEN*

SITE CONDITIONS

This example is at the opposite end of the spectrum in terms of physical size and conditions, and the list of needs and desires. A stroll garden is one in which several garden types are incorporated within the same plot. The garden is viewed from various positions within the house, from various structures in the garden itself, or while walking along its paths. The main physical conditions are as follows:

- A large backyard garden of about 25 by 15 yards (22.9 by 13.7 m). For the design that means a lot of possibilities, but also a large budget and the need for a sufficient amount of time for design and construction.
- Neighbors' properties border three sides, with the main house on the fourth side. There are a number of implications for the design relating particularly to where enclosures are used and what type of enclosures they are. Regulations on building walls and fences need to be checked, and some communities will prohibit such enclosures within a certain distance of the property line or limit their height.
- A basically level surface with several large trees near the left

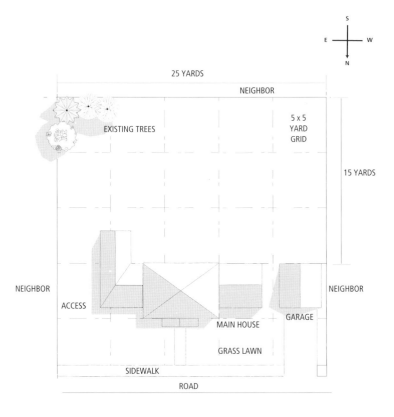

PLAN DRAWING OF LARGE GARDEN.

The large plaza of this research center in Ibaraki, north of Tokyo, is transformed into a symbolic journey from isolation to camaraderie by internationally renown garden designer and Soto Zen priest Masuno Shunmyo. Not a stroll garden in the classic sense, it shares the same purpose of revitalizing and restoring the spirit of the wandering visitor.

corner. This implies that artificial changes of ground level may be needed for some features, and existing trees will probably need to be incorporated in the new design.

- Generally good soil. The back of the house faces south. For areas with severe winters, it will be necessary to consider how snowfall and freezing conditions will affect the garden, including any underground water or drainage lines, pumps, or fishponds.
- Reasonable access for heavy equipment, diggers, or trucks. For the design, this means the ability to bring in equipment for large features such as waterfalls that might require cement retaining walls, or flatbeds and cranes for transporting and placing large stones. It also implies the need to create large features toward the back of the property and remove heavy equipment before enclosing the garden.

NEEDS AND DESIRES

Once the general physical conditions are considered, let's draw up a wish list that fully utilizes the size of the lot:

- The garden should have multiple functions: a small-scale artificial mountain/stroll garden with enough space to walk about and enjoy sitting beneath the trees; a somewhat separated tea garden with a teahouse or gazebo for entertaining family and friends; and a Zen-inspired stone-and-sand garden for spending quiet moments alone.
- Good views from the house
- A small pond for its surface reflections and cooling atmosphere
- A waterfall to feed the pond and generate soothing sounds
- A stone waterbasin (*tsukubai*) for washing the hands, and stone lanterns for light
- Some other touches, such as stepping stones and bamboo fences, to create a distinctive Japanese garden atmosphere
- Adequate distance from neighbors' properties and restricted access from the front garden and the street side of the house

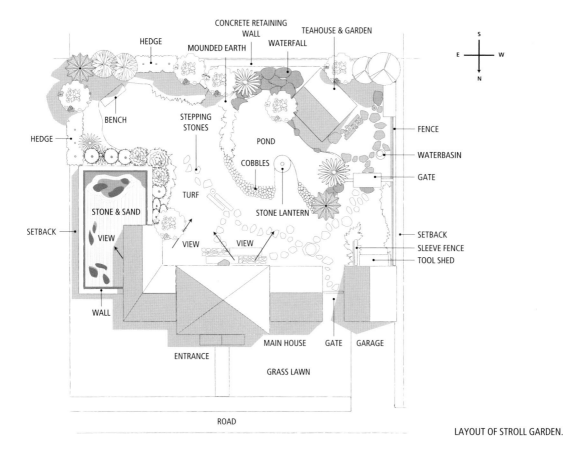

LAYOUT OF STROLL GARDEN.

Labels in the diagram:
CONCRETE RETAINING WALL · TEAHOUSE & GARDEN · HEDGE · MOUNDED EARTH · WATERFALL · S · E · W · N · BENCH · STEPPING STONES · FENCE · HEDGE · POND · WATERBASIN · COBBLES · GATE · SETBACK · STONE & SAND · VIEW · TURF · STONE LANTERN · VIEW · VIEW · VIEW · SETBACK · SLEEVE FENCE · TOOL SHED · WALL · MAIN HOUSE · GATE · GARAGE · ENTRANCE · GRASS LAWN · ROAD

GENERAL PRINCIPLES OF GARDEN DESIGN

Now that the basic conditions have been outlined, let's keep in mind a number of factors that affect the final layout. As with the design principles of the Japanese garden listed earlier, this list will apply in varying degrees to gardens of all sizes:

- The direction of the light and where we might need shade
- Related to the direction and level of light is the issue of where to put plantings that thrive in strong light and where to put those that need a cool, moist environment
- Views from within the garden and from the house (in a sitting position) along with how best to hide and reveal these views
- Relationship to adjacent properties and buildings
- Relationship to near or distant views, if any, or the need to block out unsightly surroundings
- Inlets and outlets for water, drainage, and electricity
- The location of artificial lighting for evening viewing and safety

BASIC PLAN FOR A LARGE STROLL GARDEN

After roughly tracing the ground plan, including the position of the house, and considering the elements already listed, two factors are immediately apparent. First, in order to create a proper setting and suitable atmosphere for the teahouse/gazebo, it should be situated as far away from the main house as possible. Second, to take advantage of the benefits of meditation or solitary time alone associated with the stone-and-sand garden, we want to locate it on the more private side of the house. From there it is a simple conclusion that the pond and waterfall should be grouped close to the teahouse/gazebo to increase the "mountain retreat" effect, and to keep some open foreground space for easy movement around the house. This arrangement automatically creates an asymmetrical layout while satisfying the conditions of a slightly removed tea garden on the "distant" shore of the pond, plus enough room to walk around and sit under the trees, as well as good views from the house.

This example gives some idea of the possibility of combining various garden types and functions in a surprisingly simple and natural way. Yet there remain any number of additional elements and layout possibilities, many of which will be discussed further during the course of this book.

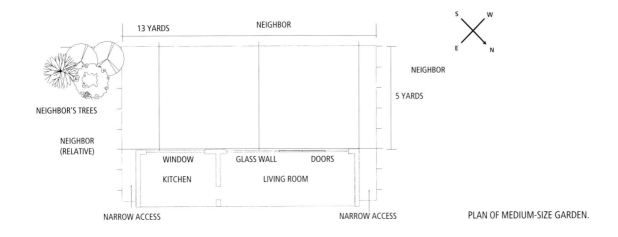

NEIGHBOR

13 YARDS

NEIGHBOR'S TREES

NEIGHBOR
(RELATIVE)

NEIGHBOR

5 YARDS

WINDOW   GLASS WALL   DOORS

KITCHEN   LIVING ROOM

NARROW ACCESS   NARROW ACCESS

PLAN OF MEDIUM-SIZE GARDEN.

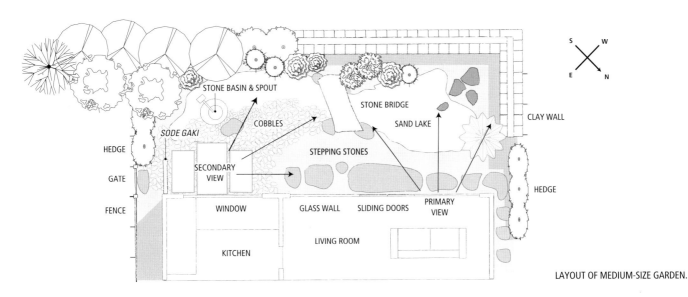

STONE BASIN & SPOUT

SODE GAKI   COBBLES

STONE BRIDGE

SAND LAKE

CLAY WALL

HEDGE

STEPPING STONES

GATE

SECONDARY
VIEW

FENCE

HEDGE

WINDOW   GLASS WALL   SLIDING DOORS

PRIMARY
VIEW

KITCHEN

LIVING ROOM

LAYOUT OF MEDIUM-SIZE GARDEN.

A MEDIUM-SIZE STONE-AND-SAND GARDEN—*KARE SANSUI*

I have saved the medium-size example for last in order to take a look at it in more detail. As before, we will start with our lists of site conditions and personal needs. After that, we will take a closer look at how to go about applying some of the basic Japanese garden design principles.

SITE CONDITIONS

The medium-size plot is best suited to one type of garden, although practical elements (a table and seating, for example) can be included to accommodate various needs. This size garden is very much within reach of the average person—with a little help from friends—to design, construct, and maintain:

- A plot of 13 yards wide by 5 yards (11.9 by 4.5 m) deep on the back side of the house with access mainly from a living room with a floor-to-ceiling sash and sliding glass doors. This implies that the garden will be viewed from the most often-used room in the house. It also implies that, with such a large expanse of glass, privacy is a concern.
- The left rear corner is due south and the right corner due west. This implies that sunlight is strong most of the day and spectacular sunsets are visible from the garden.
- Neighboring gardens border three sides, and the garden is highly visible from all these sides. The neighbor on the east side is a close relative. This implies a need for solid enclosures on the right and back side of the garden with some access to the neighbor on the left.
- The lot is in an urban setting, and any runoff rain water must be channeled into the city sewer system, while any water use will be from city water. For the design, this implies reducing construction and operating costs by exploring the use of waterless Japanese garden features.

Oceans and mountains are effectively conjured with raked sand, stone, and shaped hedge in this garden by Oguchi Motomi that evokes an image of a far away sea coast.

NEEDS AND DESIRES

Now comes our wish list:

- A private space that creates a real "escape" within the urban environment
- A garden that can be enjoyed from the adjacent room and from an exterior patio
- A garden that is not too difficult to maintain nor too costly to build
- A complete closure on the back and right side, but some ease of access to the relative's property on the left
- A calm and peaceful space to enjoy alone or with family and friends

GENERAL PRINCIPLES OF GARDEN DESIGN

We will start again with a rough-dimension plan showing the garden, house, and neighboring lots. In this space we have decided to create a garden that will be primarily viewed from inside the adjacent living room. However, we also feel the need for a minimal outdoor patio area designed in keeping with the sensibilities of the Japanese garden. A stone-and-sand garden fits well with the site conditions and the type of garden we hope to achieve.

The tranquility and private nature of the garden we have in mind demands a solid enclosure to keep disturbances to a minimum and prying eyes out. For this purpose we'll use a traditional Japanese clay wall (*dobei*) topped with a coping of Japanese roof tiles for the back and the right side of the garden that border our neighbors' properties. For the left side of the garden that is adjacent to a relative's plot, we will use shrubs to form a hedge for about two-thirds of the length, and a lightweight bamboo fence—plus a simple gate—for the remaining one-third. This will provide adequate isolation while allowing easy access to either property. The addition of a bamboo "sleeve fence" (*sode gaki*) around one corner of the patio will lend added privacy.

We start the layout by deciding the location of the patio area. The patio has functional needs that will best be met by locating it next to the house in order to limit movement through the garden. Since the doors for entering the garden are on the right side of the house, the patio will be located on the left. Now we have two primary garden-viewing points: inside the house on the right and from the patio on the left.

MEDIUM-SIZE GARDEN, PERSPECTIVE VIEW.

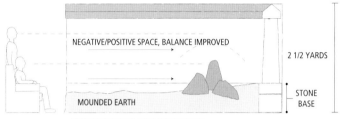

STANDING EYE LEVEL, 5–6 FEET

SEATED EYE LEVEL, 3–4 FEET

GROUPING LOOKS TOO SMALL, WALL TOO LARGE

NEGATIVE/POSITIVE SPACE, BALANCE IMPROVED

2 1/2 YARDS

STONE BASE

MOUNDED EARTH

GROUPING LOOKS LARGE, MORE VISIBLE

MOUNDING EARTH TO CREATE A BETTER VIEW.

That implies a main visual focus toward the right rear corner of the garden. We have also noted the need for solid enclosures at the back and on the right side of the garden that fit well with this focal point. With the left side of the garden adjacent to a relative's garden, we want to plant that side and corner most heavily to take advantage of the neighbor's leafy garden and give them the advantage of ours—in effect doubling the size of our little "forest."

Continuing in this manner—by taking our cues from existing conditions and practical considerations and coupling them with our desires and Japanese garden design principles—we soon arrive at the finished layout shown here. In this example, a small stone grouping will occupy a prime visual position, but it could just as well be a sculpture, stone lantern, a tree, or even empty space. The waterbasin is located near the patio area, from where water can be easily sprinkled around the patio and hands conveniently washed. A stone lantern could be located slightly behind and higher than the waterbasin to shed light on this area. A simpler alternative is a portable light, candles, or spotlights attached to the wall of the house at about the second-floor level and aimed at this spot. Water can be run to the basin with a traditional Japanese bamboo and pipe

Earth is mounded and planted in front of this bamboo fence, and a large, standing stone is arranged with several smaller ones. The shape of the mound and use of cobblestones to fill the front side of the slope seem to lift the standing stone and heighten its importance.

arrangement. By having an additional spout on the water inlet pipe at the bottom rear of the waterbasin, a hose can be conveniently attached for watering trees and plantings. From the spillover of the waterbasin flows a symbolic river and pond made of raked gravel, with a wooden or stone bridge and "island" stone set into the sea of gravel. (An actual drain should be located at the base of the waterbasin and disguised with pebbles or cobblestones as discussed in detail in chapter 4.) Stepping stones (*tobi ishi*) turn left and right from the entrance to the house, ending at the patio and waterbasin on the left, and wrapping around the house to a side gate on the right.

Before moving on to preparations for construction, I should mention that there is really no such thing as a finished layout or plan when it comes to traditional Japanese garden construction. For one reason, the final outcome of the garden is very dependent on the natural materials that compose it. Final judgments cannot be made until you have the actual rocks, plants, and other materials in hand. Site conditions are another fact of nature that may not be known until site work begins (for example, you might find a large hidden boulder just where you expected to dig a hole). Building a garden is more akin to cooking or painting than it is to building a house. With the actual materials in hand, the gardener may decide to change the number of elements or adjust the placements

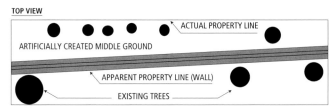

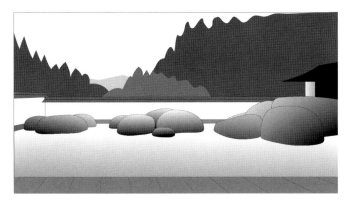

EXAMPLE OF "BORROWED SCENERY." The diminishing size and placement of the shrubs echoes the perspective of the trees in the distance visually connecting the two. Based on the garden at Shoden-ji, Kyoto, Japan.

EXAMPLE OF CREATING A MIDDLE GROUND. A low wall can be set in front of the actual property line and several straight-trunk trees planted to create an artificial middle-ground and a sense of connection between the garden and the distant landscape. Based on an image of Furumine shrine, Ibaraki, Japan.

in response to a dialogue that develops between him and the garden as it takes shape. Although the gardener will have a main theme in mind (either a literary, symbolic, or formal design), and will not change that theme as he goes along, a plan is still a road map and not a destination. The destination depends on your reaction to developments along the way, as well as on what happens when your creative instincts kick in. This differs greatly from the approach of landscape architects and architects who must provide customers and contractors with fixed and detailed plans.

Up until now we have been looking only at our plan view in two dimensions, but in reality we have been thinking in three dimensions. Let's look at some other views to better understand the Japanese approach to the layout and enclosure of the garden.

Taking a look at a view of the corner containing the stone grouping (page 31), we'll project the drawing vertically to approximate heights. Assuming a seated position from a couch within the adjacent room, we see that the eye level of a seated person will be between 3 and 4 feet (90 and 120 cm) high. The eye level of the same person in a standing position will be 5 to 6 feet (150 to 180 cm) high. This shows us very clearly that in order to view grouped objects as we expect, the ground level on which they sit will need to be adjusted. In fact, this is one device used in Japanese gardens to allow distant elements in the garden to be viewed more easily. The idea is similar to displaying items on a shelf. In order to see the rear items clearly, they need to sit on a raised base. Creating artificial hills, especially at the far side of the garden, is a classic method of adding visual interest in Japanese gardens while allowing the most distant objects to be easily seen.

Another aspect of three-dimensional design involves the relationship of the garden to its surrounding environment—the Japanese design principle known as *shakkei*, or "borrowed scenery." This is the idea that the eye does not stop at the boundary of the garden but simultaneously takes in everything around, beyond, and above it. There are a number of techniques the gardener uses to integrate his garden with the existing scene, many of them similar to techniques used by painters. Like a painter, the gardener considers the foreground, middle ground, and background to create a complete image. Unlike the painter, the gardener can determine neither the middle ground nor the background outside his garden—they are givens with which he must work. Instead, he lays out his garden in such a way that the middle ground and background seem to exist to accommodate his garden.

One way to do this is by using a technique referred to in painting terms as "echo." The shapes of distant trees or mountains may be echoed in the shapes and types of plantings in the garden. Colors of flowering trees in the distance may be echoed with similar flowering trees or shrubs in the garden. Or certain natural rhythms or repetitions of shapes may be picked up and repeated within the garden proper. This is by no means an attempt to mimic the landscape. It is a careful composing of a close-up foreground with all the depth of nature itself.

Another technique is to create a shallow middle ground to act as a transition to the more distant background. In this case, the garden enclosure may actually be placed within the property boundary so as to create a shallow intermediary space that appears to be outside the garden but is actually within the control of the garden designer.

ENCLOSURES ▶

1. Clay walls (*dobei*): **A**. A wood frame with horizontal bamboo poles is completely filled and covered with a mixture of clay and straw (see also page 36). **B**. A rough wooden frame, open at the base, is fitted with a bamboo lattice that is coated with a clay-and-straw mixture. Both types are covered with a tile or cedar shingle roof.

2. Wooden walls (*itabei*): **A**. Wide vertical boards are nailed to a wooden frame which is visible on the back side. **B**. Wide boards are alternated on either side of the frame. Both types are covered with a tile or cedar shingle roof and may or may not be braced on the back side.

3. Tea-whisk (*chasen*) fences: **A**. Rough wood posts and a wooden frame support vertical bundles of bush clover, bamboo with the leaves still attached, or other straight, narrow branches. Each bundle is between 3 and 4 inches (7 and 10 cm) in diameter, tied with wire, and secured to the wood frame. Bamboo, whole or split, is secured horizontally across the front and back with rope. **B**. Bundles in a tea-whisk shape about 8 inches (20 cm) in diameter and bound with wire are hung from bamboo poles. This type is most often used as a sleeve fence. Both types leave one end of the bundle unbound to form the head of the whisk. The roof is separated from the top of the whisks by 4 to 8 inches (10 to 20 cm).

4. *Katsura gaki* fences: **A**. A wooden frame and plywood wall is constructed. Narrow bamboo with the leaves attached is tightly stacked and laid vertically against the plywood. The branches are folded behind the main stem, gradually concealing the plywood base. Split bamboo strips are run horizontally and nailed in place to secure the bamboo. **B**. Bamboo branches are stacked horizontally and the wall finished with whole-bamboo poles.

5. *Koetsu* sleeve fence (*Koetsu sode gaki*): This fence features a diagonal, open-weave of single or double bamboo poles.

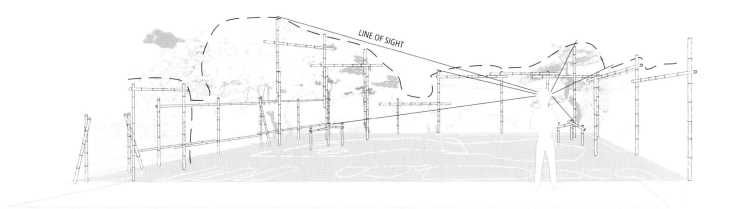

CHECKING THE GENERAL HEIGHT OF PLANNED OBJECTS, USING DIFFERENT LENGTHS OF BAMBOO.

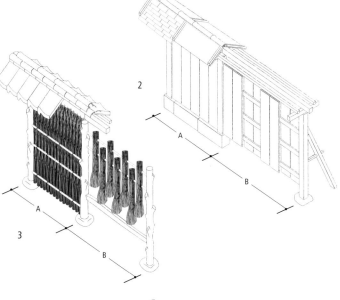

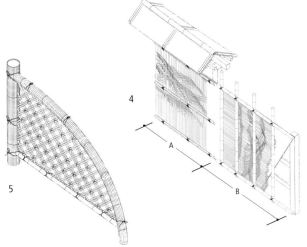

PRACTICE

With our layout sheet in hand, we'll proceed to transpose our layout onto the ground by drawing lines with white sand or limestone. Starting with the placement of the clay wall and the patio, we'll layout our main features: marking the waterbasin near the patio, then outlining the gravel pond in an irregular pattern. Next, we'll locate the stone grouping on the far side of the dry pond.

Continue like this, mapping out the placement for the bridge, the stone in the pond, the "shoe-removal" stone (*kutsunugi ishi*), and the stepping stones, and finally the trees, bushes, and hedges along the perimeter. When that's done, we'll step back and take a look from our main viewing points (and maybe the second floor of the house, too, if possible).

After checking the placement of all the elements in our layout, checking the relative height of the objects will help us visualize and adjust the planned garden in three dimensions. As an aid to visualization, we can take some bamboo or wooden poles of various lengths and paint markings on them at one-foot (30-cm) intervals. (Count an extra foot at the bottom for inserting the pole in the ground.) Stand them in the proposed garden area in the approximate positions and at the approximate heights of the elements as you know them to be. Then sit and stand in the expected viewing positions to get a better sense of the relation of the elements to each other and to objects outside the garden. The height of the pole can be quickly adjusted by driving it farther into the ground, or by taping two poles together to extend the length. This is one way to decide whether you might need more height to obstruct something you don't want to see or whether some object might need to be raised to keep it from being obscured. Modify your plan as needed.

ENCLOSURES

As mentioned at the beginning of this chapter, the size and shape of the garden imply a critically important aspect: How should the garden be enclosed? Basic enclosures in Japanese gardens include hedges, clay walls, bamboo fences, stone walls, and wooden fences. Wooden fences are generally constructed by carpenters under the supervision

1

2

3

4

5

6

7

8

9

of the gardener. Japanese gardeners are proficient in the other four types, although stone walls will sometimes require specialists.

The degree of the garden's integration with, and isolation from, the surrounding environment is a carefully planned and controlled design consideration of the Japanese garden. One important part of the garden designer's work is choosing the right type of enclosure to achieve the best relationship between the house, the surrounding environment, and the garden.

For instance, the low, straight, and relatively textureless wall often found surrounding the stone-and-sand garden does little to compete with rock arrangements and raked sand that are the main feature of this type of garden. Yet this enclosure, whether of natural brown clay mixed with plant fibers or coated with white plaster, provides just the right amount of isolation needed to keep distracting movement outside the garden from interfering with contemplation, at the same time allowing tall greenery outside the wall to form part of the garden's backdrop.

A stone footing can add a sense of strength and permanence to an enclosure, while creating a transition between the man-made structure and the supporting earth. In fact, in a country where wooden construction is the norm, and where rainfall is high, wooden-post construction of buildings as well as of fences almost always relies on stone supports to reduce wood rot. This very practical consideration is thus the root of a very Japanese aesthetic. Clay walls, for example, always employ a base of stone to protect them from standing water.

In other cases, a full and neatly trimmed hedge may be equally effective. This option provides a softer touch and the potential for the added surprise of seasonal flowers.

Bamboo fences are closely associated with the Japanese garden and are probably one of the most

A VARIETY OF ENCLOSURES.

1. Stacked and cut spicebush (*kuromoji*) branches secured with split bamboo and covered with a wood plank roof (not shown).

2. Slender bamboo branches, with the leaves attached and folded underneath, over a plywood base, secured with strips of split bamboo.

3. Sleeve fence composed of several different diameters of bamboo in front of a fence of bamboo in a checkerboard pattern.

4. Variation of a *Koetsu* sleeve fence with diagonal bamboo running in one direction rather than crossed.

5 "Drift" style (*fukiyose*) sleeve fence.

6. A "diamond weave" fence, using a bamboo lattice and wooden-pole frame.

7. A thick wall composed of clay and stacked roofing tiles (*neribei*) and topped with roofing tiles (*kawara*).

8. Clay mixed with various grades of sand and some cement, rammed into a wooden form which is then removed.

9. A stonewall made of volcanic tuff (*shiro ishi* or *oya ishi*). Notice the difference between older and newer stone where the wall has been repaired.

Left: An attractive and inventive three-story curtain wall of stainless steel and wood strips by Osaka architect Takehara Yoshiji carries reflected light from the open, third floor ceiling down to the basement level. *Right*: This bamboo and wood frame fence by Nagasaka Dai provides a beautiful face of natural materials to harmonize with the street while lending a backdrop of flickering light to the front garden of this Kyoto house.

attractive and varied enclosures ever created. The sheer number of styles, techniques, and names associated with bamboo fences attests to their long history. A sampling of attractive types is included here. Once you have chosen a suitable style, you can consider whether to purchase a ready-made product or make your own. Many books can be found on how to construct them, with step-by-step procedures and instructions for tying the numerous knots associated with the black or brown rope (*shuronawa*) that is used to hold them together.

Bamboo fences are used both as boundaries and as decorative space dividers known as *sode gaki*, or "sleeve fences," because they were said to look like the sleeves of a kimono. When used as a space divider to block or redirect the line of vision, this type of fence is generally about 2 yards high by 1 to 1 1/2 yards wide and is often affixed to the side of a building at a ninety-degree angle. A shorter, wider free-standing version is used to provide a backdrop to a group of plantings, stone lantern, stone waterbasin, or a combination of these elements. In this setting, a *Koetsu gaki* fence, with one end curving into the ground, is often employed.

Another common, though nontraditional, use of bamboo fences is as a screening device to disguise unsightly or inappropriate walls that, for one reason or another, cannot be removed (similar to our veranda wall example). Especially in urban environments, where neighboring walls are shared or where "maintenance-free" aluminum fences are in abundance, bamboo is quite often used as a lightweight, inexpensive, and attractive "wall within a wall."

In this chapter we have looked at layout and garden design and the related subject of enclosures. Before taking a closer look at the use of stone in the garden, we'll have one final lesson, from a gardener with forty years' experience, on how to construct one type of Japanese-style clay wall.

BUILDING A TRADITIONAL CLAY WALL IN THE *NURU* STYLE
by Yasumoro Sadao

Japanese clay walls (*dobei*) can be classified into three basic types: *tsumu*, *kizuku*, and *nuru*. The *tsumu* style is composed of bricks of sun-dried clay cemented together with the same clay mixture. The *kizuku* style consists of creating a form with thick boards or poles and compacting clay between them, after which the boards are removed. One variation of the third type, the *nuru* style, is described below.

YASUMORO SADAO has been a garden designer (*niwashi*) for over forty years. A native of Machida, a suburb of Tokyo, he studied as a high school student under several famous garden critics and teachers, after which he traveled around the country for three or four years, studying most of Japan's famous gardens. He then returned to Tokyo and was apprenticed to the master gardener Saito Katsuo for about fifteen years before setting up on his own.

—— *"I always use materials found at the site or on nearby mountains. In this way I can create a garden that best suits the local environment and at the same time minimizes waste. For me, creating a garden is not about previously decided methods and materials, nor is it about religion or philosophy. For me it is just about using one's own energy and skill to create something to be enjoyed. Even maintenance is not a question of perfection but of care for a natural environment where weeds exist alongside moss. While listening to the kami (gods) living at the site, and bearing in mind the feelings of the owner, I begin to work. In the case of a tea garden for example, differences in the owner's approach to tea need to be respected, and this influences how the garden will be constructed. But even then, one should never be so serious so as to create a garden design devoid of deep emotion. Most important of all is to put your heart into your work."*

1

1

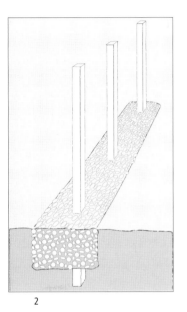

2

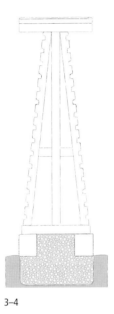

3–4

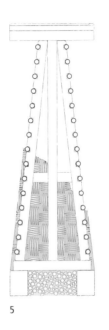

5

5

5

1. The clay-and-straw mixture, which makes up the bulk of the *nuru* wall, is mixed in stages as the work progresses by cutting straw or some other strong grass into 4- to 6-inch (10- to 15-cm) lengths and mixing it into the clay and water until it is a pasty mass. Just about any clay-rich soil will do as long as you knead it with the water and straw until it is sticky.

2. Dig a 12-inch (30-cm) deep trench the length and width of the base of the wall (no less than 20 inches [50 cm] wide for a 2-yard-high wall). Fill the trench with a damp mix of gravel, clay, and lime. Dig a 2-foot (60-cm) hole every 2 yards for the main posts, which should be about 4 x 4 inches by 2 1/2 yards (10 x 10 cm by 2.5 m). Tamp down the gravel, clay, and lime into the trench while spraying it lightly with water, and let this solidify after checking that the posts are aligned and straight.

3. Set the stones for the base of the wall. There are many ways to do this but the simplest way is to use straight-cut stone. Line up the stones, then backfill and tamp down the same gravel, clay, and lime slag between the stones. The total stone height should be at least 8 inches (20 cm) to protect the base of the wall from sitting in water.

4. Construct the frame as shown using two-by-fours and long wood screws. Be sure the bottom is firmly resting on the stone. The wall tapers toward the top at a ratio of 1 in 10 (a 10% slope) and the frame is notched to receive the bamboo poles (unnotched frames and split bamboo can also be used). Horizontal boards connect the frames at the top and form a base for split bamboo, tied together with rope.

5. Drill holes in the bamboo poles and nail them in place to complete the frame. Mount the bamboo from the bottom up and slowly backfill with the clay-and-straw mixture as you go. Trowel the same clay-and-straw mix over the entire surface (or just spread it with your hands) until the bamboo poles peek through only here and there. Coat the top of the structure and the cut bamboo with this mix. You can add sand and use short, chopped straw in a final surfacing mix if you want a finer surface. The wall will take two months or more to dry completely, so it should not be constructed in the winter or any time when water is in danger of freezing during the lengthy drying period. Oil can be mixed with the final surface clay to make a harder, more waterproof surface.

6. Screw 10- to 12-inch x 1-inch (25- to 30-cm x 2.5-cm) boards to the top to form a base for the coping. The coping is usually made of ceramic tiles (*meita kawara*), or cypress shingles over an exterior plywood base. The tile is nailed on and the final coping tile is wired in place at the peak. Be sure to extend the coping sufficiently to allow rain runoff to miss the base of the wall, as well as provide visual balance. The total height of the clay wall should not exceed about 2 yards.

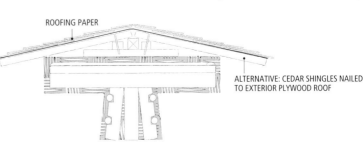

UPPER TILES AND CAP ANCHORED WITH WIRE TO PIPE

STEEL PIPE ANCHORED WITH WIRE NAILED TO TOP BOARD

RUNOFF

ROOFING PAPER

ALTERNATIVE: CEDAR SHINGLES NAILED TO EXTERIOR PLYWOOD ROOF

6

CHAPTER 3

STONE-AND-SAND GARDENS

The ephemeral qualities of light and the interplay of nature with manmade surfaces are but a few of the temporal actors on a mutable stage, captured for moments at a time in this courtyard garden by Sasaki Yoji in collaboration with architect Sakamoto Akira.

A dry garden on the fourth floor of the Canadian embassy in Tokyo by Zen priest Masuno Shunmyo employees formal tensions and the close proximity of the two halves of a split bolder to symbolize the character of Japan and the ties between countries.

In this chapter we will focus on the uses of stone in the Japanese garden and especially the Zen-influenced stone-and-sand gardens known as *kare sansui*.

"In all the world, it is only the Japanese who have removed flowers from the garden," says garden designer and tea master Oguchi Motomi, whose work appears in this book. The construction of a garden with only stone and sand is unique to Japan and is the result of the intense emphasis on searching for deeper experience that was the hallmark of Zen acolytes and those they influenced from the thirteenth century onward.

The special place of importance occupied by stone in the Japanese psyche certainly predates Zen. As we have seen in Chapter 1, the native Shinto religion reveres large stones as dwelling places of the gods, and, though probably unrelated to Shinto, evidence of stone arrangements date to the Oyu stone circles in Akita Prefecture in northern Japan, manmade arrangements dating to the late Jomon period (2,500–1,000 B.C.).

From at least the tenth century, the term *ishi o tateru*, or "the placing or arranging of stones," was closely associated with the very meaning of garden-making. This may be because, at the early stage of the craft, placing stones and building water features such as ponds, streams, and waterfalls was of greater importance than plantings. Stones—and water displays that prominently feature stone—were strongly connected to the form of the garden, and even today stone placement is referred to as the "bone structure" of the garden.

The expression *ishitate-so* means, literally, "stone-arranging priest." The expression refers to a class of garden-making priests originally associated with the Shingon and Tendai sects of Buddhism, specifically those connected to the temple of Ninnaji in Kyoto. But it was not until Chinese Song-dynasty landscape painting employing only black ink converged with the Zen search for the true or "original" self that the austere beauty of the stone-and-sand garden was born.

Islands have always played a central role in Japanese garden design in both a functional and symbolic sense. The bridges link island to shore in a physical sense and represent the idea of "crossing over" in a spiritual sense. Direct links between materials and meaning are common in the Japanese garden and the knowledge and use of symbolic forms continue to be a yardstick by which even modern gardeners measure the depth of a design.

The stone-and-sand garden is generally viewed while seated inside an adjacent room or on a veranda, or from the edge of the garden. Viewers do not enter or walk though it. This aspect is essential to its design. Another aspect relates to the division of Zen meditation into *zazen* (sitting meditation) and *samu* (working meditation), the latter of which relates to garden maintenance. The Zen-style garden usually incorporates a layer of gravel 3 to 6 inches (8 to 15 cm) deep, which is maintained by daily raking. The wide pitch of the wooden rake and the sharp edges of the gravel will help to maintain the raked hills and troughs even over a period of weeks. Leaf and other debris accumulate more quickly, especially in fall, and there is no way to remove them without walking on the raked surface. Whether the daily raking is a necessity, or whether a consistent work routine has value on a spiritual plane, depends on the motivation of the gardener.

Before you decide to create a stone-and-sand garden you should of course consider the type and frequency of maintenance required. However, while any style of garden requires maintenance, keeping a garden pristine is less of a goal than the cleansing effects on the mind and soul that accrue from maintaining a physical and metaphysical order on one small patch of earth.

If you do create a Zen-style garden, you might begin as we did in Chapter 2. Let's return to the large layout and concentrate on the stone-and-sand garden area already depicted.

In this layout, the stone-and-sand garden is adjacent to a den that will primarily be used by the adults in the house. We are assuming that a good part of the wall facing the garden is floor-to-ceiling glass or contains large glass doors. This layout also assumes some overhang of the eaves providing a minimum of shade in the room and shelter from the rain even with the doors open.

Looking at the drawing, the garden enclosure considered here is a clay wall such as the one described at the end of Chapter 2. The height is slightly above eye level (about 2 yards) and set forward enough to allow rain runoff to fall on this side of the property line. There is a danger that rain or runoff water from the eaves of the building will disperse or spoil the garden sand. One way of avoiding this is to use small round pebbles (*kuri ishi*) laid in a strip around the edge of the garden next to the wall and under the edges of the eaves. This affords protection from sudden bursts of runoff water falling from above and prevents the formation of puddles or the scattering of the lighter gravel. Black pebbles known as *nachiguro* are often used for this purpose. The pebbles are placed within a

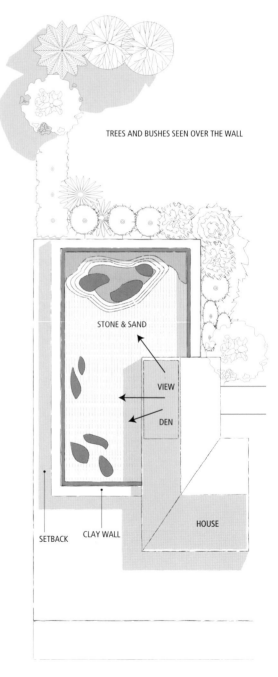

TREES AND BUSHES SEEN OVER THE WALL

STONE & SAND

VIEW

DEN

HOUSE

SETBACK   CLAY WALL

STONE-AND-SAND GARDEN FROM THE LARGE STROLL GARDEN LAYOUT.

BORDER STONES AND OTHER STONE DETAILS.

1. A symbolic refuse hole (*chiriana*) cut into cement mixed with small pebbles and filled with granite stones.

2. A symphony of stone ground work, inlaid stone, and foundation stones under wood columns.

3. Fine white gravel, larger rough gravel, and stone edging—all of them granite—flanked by a walk-way of bamboo.

4. Haircup moss, stone, and cobblestones are bordered by a double row of inlaid roof tiles

strip between the sand and the enclosing wall, and the sand and the eaves of the house. The pebbles are held in place within long, square-cut edging stones or Japanese roof tiles known as *kawara*. The *kawara* are buried on their side with enough of the tiles projecting from the ground to separate the gravel from the pebbles. The shape of the *kawara* lends itself to being laid in a straight line while providing an interesting, slightly decorative edge. In fact, *kawara* are often used to lend a patterned effect to exterior ground surfacing. Old *kawara* are commonly stacked in combination with clay to create walls known as *neribei*.

Referring again to our drawing, we see that there are only four elements: the clay wall, the raked gravel, the stone settings, and some ground cover. Your own design may involve some other features such as plantings, areas of grass or moss, mounds of earth, or even more elaborate stone settings meant to represent an aspect of nature such as a waterfall. Dry waterfalls often play a role in stone-and-sand gardens, and at the end of this chapter we show how you can construct one. In this book you will also find a large number of dry gardens that incorporate plantings and other features in new and interesting ways.

Before going on to the specifics of what rocks to pick or where to set them in the garden, let's take a moment to think about what we are trying to achieve.

A Zen-style garden is not necessarily for the purpose of meditation in the strict sense of the word. Besides the previously mentioned benefits of working meditation, we are looking for the kind of space in which the mind can expand with a feeling of tranquility, not unlike the mesmerizing and calming effect of gazing out at the sea. Indeed, the imagery associated with the Zen garden is often the ocean, with rocks taking on the role of distant islands, mountains, or objects moving through the sea (although associations with the universe and other imagery are equally valid). As with a painting, the mind of the observer completes the image, "filling in the blanks" with original ideas and reflections. In this respect, it may be helpful to remember the words of the American artist Jasper Johns, who said, "Sometimes I see a thing and then I paint it. Sometimes I paint it and then I see it."

More than specific imagery, a sense of the historic precedents and the cultural context in which the stone-and-sand garden has evolved, coupled with your own experience and sensitivities, will give you the necessary grasp of what to look for. Whatever symbolic meaning ultimately emerges should do so naturally and is secondary to a satisfying design.

The art of the Zen garden is one that evolved in tandem with a spiritual imperative to eschew the irrelevant and transient in favor of the essential, enduring truths of nature. This is not to say that sensual beauty is not present, but neither is it the goal. Certainly in a garden with so few elements—raked gravel, a few well-placed stones, and some moss, as in the garden of Ryoanji in Kyoto—sensual beauty has been reduced, like the Mona Lisa, to the faintest smile.

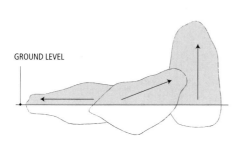

GROUND LEVEL

VERTICAL, HORIZONTAL, AND DIAGONAL MOVEMENT
INHERENT IN THE SHAPE AND PLACEMENT OF A STONE.

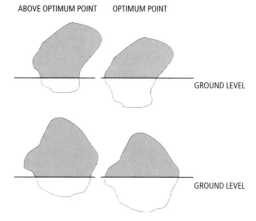

ABOVE OPTIMUM POINT   OPTIMUM POINT

GROUND LEVEL

GROUND LEVEL

APPEARANCE OF STABILITY RELATED TO THE OPTIMUM BURIAL
POINT OF THE STONE.

STONE BASICS

The selection and setting of the stones is one of the most difficult aspects of garden-making. Large stones may be costly, and the total expense to move and set them can be substantial. *The Journal of Japanese Gardening*, an American bimonthly, recommends procuring the stones early, if it is not the first step, in your garden-making process even if the additional expense means you have to delay other purchases. This is good advice for those who have made a commitment to develop their garden over a long period of time. As the magazine points out, deciding to bring in large stones after the garden is set will cause disruption and extra expense. Generally, if stones are moved in a Japanese garden after it is completed, it is as part of a total redesign since most gardens, and especially dry gardens, depend first and foremost on the placement of the stones.

For those who have not yet made such a commitment or are experimenting with their first garden, smaller stones that can be carried by two people or lifted with a small winch can still be sensitively arranged and satisfying both as an experience of the process and for the result. Be modest but undaunted in your challenge of this art. The following is a short list of fundamentals concerning the choice and setting of stones:

1. Stone has an orientation and a "face" that must be turned toward the main viewing position when it is set in place. The face is said to be the side that most expresses the character of the stone and contains no unsightly blemishes. Another factor is the matching of geological zones. In other words, stone that comes from mountains should be used with a mountain landscape image, while stone that comes from a river or riverbank should be used along the "shore" of a "pond" or "river," where its natural weathering will suit its location in the garden. Although it is not always possible to procure materials from parallel sources, try to respect the character of the stone in your design.

2. In addition to its geological zone, a stone's orientation to the earth is also important and should be maintained. If you acquire or buy the stone elsewhere, you can still identify its orientation from markings on the stone: weathering, changes in color due to how it was buried in the earth, striations, and so on will help you find the natural orientation of each stone.

3. Each stone has one or more natural directions: vertical, horizontal, or diagonal—all derived from its shape. This direction is an important factor, particularly in the composition of a group of stones.

4. Scale is an important design factor. Stones are selected with the size of the garden in mind and with an eye toward the balance between the stone and the open space surrounding it. Traditionally, large stones were not selected for small gardens where they would overwhelm the space. In modern times, however, this has been one area of change and experimentation.

Raked white sand and a massive stone "monument" impart a quiet majesty to the courtyard garden of a crematorium by garden designer Takasaki Yasutaka. The unusual band of gold leaf added to the stone surface lends a note of formality and respect to the rough gravity of the stone.

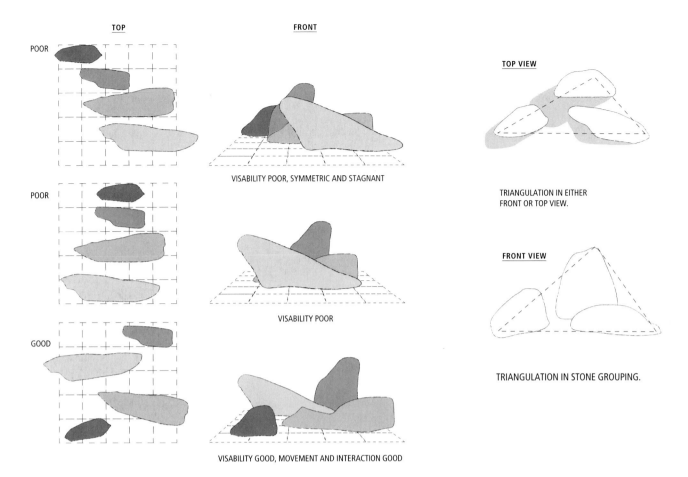

TOP   FRONT

POOR

POOR

GOOD

VISABILITY POOR, SYMMETRIC AND STAGNANT

VISABILITY POOR

VISABILITY GOOD, MOVEMENT AND INTERACTION GOOD

TOP VIEW

TRIANGULATION IN EITHER FRONT OR TOP VIEW.

FRONT VIEW

TRIANGULATION IN STONE GROUPING.

POOR AND GOOD EXAMPLES OF STONE GROUPING.

5. A stone is set in such a way that a good portion may be buried below ground. This is important to lend a visual sense of stability and naturalism to the stone setting and to insure actual stability. In deciding how much of the stone to bury, keep in mind that undercuts toward the base should be hidden to avoid the impression of fragility.

6. As with garden design in general, asymmetrical composition is the rule in stone setting. Avoid lining stones up in a row or placing them at equal intervals. Arrangements that entirely hide some stones from the primary viewing positions are to be avoided as well.

7. Triangular groupings of stone viewed both frontally and from above are the norm when three or more stones are involved. There are many reasons for this, including the impression of stability afforded by three-dimensional objects that are broad at the base and narrow at the top (mountains and pyramids are two such forms), as well as a clearer sense of visual hierarchy formed by groups of small, medium, and large stones. Another reason is that irregular triangles create a direction—like an arrow—which can be used subtly to direct the eye around the garden. This does not involve strict geometric composition, which is almost never adopted, but lines of force and tension. Some classic examples of triangular stone groupings are listed in the section below.

8. The Japanese preference for color in stone traditionally leans toward grays, reddish browns, and green-blues (such as chlorite schist). White or black stones were seldom used, except as pebbles and cobblestones. This was especially true in Zen gardens, where the ground is generally a light-colored gravel. Combinations of stones with strongly contrasting colors were also rarely used. This is another area that has undergone some change in modern times.

9. Historically, cut or polished stones were avoided. However, the concept of taking something from its original context and "reinventing" it by placing it in a new context was an exception pioneered by the originators of the tea garden. Known as *mitate* in Japanese, this results in stones previously used for other purposes—such as disc-shaped millstones or other shaped stones taken from demolished buildings—being recycled as elements in the garden. Millstones, for example, are commonly laid flat and used as stepping stones.

Buddhist doctrines of impermanence and emptiness tinged the aesthetic of refined beauty (*miyabi*) with a note of sadness and resignation. This more somber aesthetic called *mono no aware* (perhaps best understood as "poignancy"), is clearly expressed in this Buddhist triad grouping (*sanzon seki*) by garden designer Oguchi Motomi.

However, the use of quarried and sculpted stone is one aspect of the garden that changed drastically during the twentieth century, with cut, polished, or otherwise processed and shaped specimens appearing more frequently. Although the altering of "natural" stone has a long history, in the past this was done mostly for the purpose of making stone look *more* natural in its new setting. The lack of weathered stones has fostered an industry in the artificial weathering of new stone, but the use of obviously cut or otherwise processed stone is as much a response to the postwar prevalence of modern and Western architecture as it is to the dwindling supply of natural stone.

One common method of obtaining stones in Japan is to use whatever stones are dug up at the site, augmenting them with purchased stones when necessary. This is a clear example of the need to work from instinct, as mentioned in Chapter 2, as much as from a set plan. While this method of stone collection works well in mountainous or rocky areas or in a place where gardens have previously been made and demolished, it will not be an option in areas where unearthing natural stone is unlikely.

A surer method is to take your design in hand and go looking for the stone you want. The difficulty of this process depends on where you live. It may be difficult to gather information on natural stone, and in places where weathered, moss-covered stones are not prized (as they are in Japan), you may have some difficulty in getting suppliers or acquaintances to understand your needs. Leave yourself enough time to search. When you eventually find the right stones in a quarry, a neighbor's garden, or a friend's country house, photograph each stone from all sides, then make a sketch and note down the rough dimensions. While you arrange for the stone to be transported and wait for delivery, you'll have time to modify your design, now knowing what the actual materials will look like.

STONE GROUPINGS

There are a large number of traditional groupings with their attendant symbolism that may be helpful for you to keep in mind when arranging your stones. Here are just a few of the most common groupings and their basic significance:

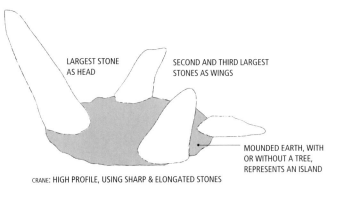

LARGEST STONE
AS HEAD

SECOND AND THIRD LARGEST
STONES AS WINGS

MOUNDED EARTH, WITH
OR WITHOUT A TREE,
REPRESENTS AN ISLAND

CRANE: HIGH PROFILE, USING SHARP & ELONGATED STONES

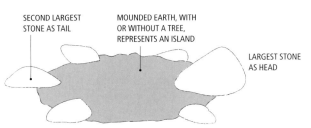

SECOND LARGEST
STONE AS TAIL

MOUNDED EARTH, WITH
OR WITHOUT A TREE,
REPRESENTS AN ISLAND

LARGEST STONE
AS HEAD

TURTLE: LOW PROFILE, USING ROUNDED STONES

STONE GROUPINGS, BASED ON MYTHOLOGICAL
AND CULTURAL THEMES.

This variation on a crane arrangement uses angular lengths of blue stone nestled under a tree in an "island" hedge.

1. Stone grouping begins with a minimum of two stones. While there are any number of ways of arranging two stones, the key is that in such a grouping one stone is always subordinate to the other. In other words, one of the two stones is obviously larger and more "important" than the other.

2. Numerical groupings of three, five, and seven. In Japanese culture three, five, and seven are auspicious or lucky numbers. The arrangement of stones in Kyoto's Ryoanji is one of the better-known examples of this type.

3. Buddhist Triad Rocks (*sanzon seki*) is an arrangement of three stones in close proximity such that the center stone is larger or stronger than the two flanking stones and the three form a triangle or triad when seen from the front or back. The name refers to the common representation of the Buddha flanked by two attendant bodhisattvas.

4. Horizontal Triad Rocks (*hinbon seki*) is another arrangement of three stones. Whereas the Buddhist Triad Rocks is an arrangement of vertical stones, *hinbon seki* is an arrangement of horizontal or "low profile" (*fuseishi*) stones that form a triangle when seen from above.

5. Heaven, Earth, and Man (*oshakei*, or *ten-chi-jin*). This is not so much a specific grouping as a symbolic systemization of natural forces related to Chinese geomancy. The vertical height represents heaven in relation to earth. Earth is represented by the lateral thrust seen in horizontal stones. The diagonal thrust is seen as active and represents man and the transmission of energy from one point to another.

6. The Crane and the Turtle (*tsuru* and *kame*). These are symbolic images and are essentially two separate stone groupings often seen together. By and large, these rock configurations are used in conjunction with islands in ponds or with plant-covered mounds of earth intended to represent an island in a dry garden. Both images symbolize good fortune and long life. In addition, the turtle is a symbol of old age and is often associated with the Taoist belief in the "Islands of the Immortals," one of which was said to be borne on the back of a large turtle. The crane, on the other hand, is often used as a symbol of youth due to the upward-facing, energetic appearance of its wings, neck, and beak.

PLACING AND GROUPING STONES

With some idea of these general rules and classic stone groupings in mind, let's look at how to go about placing stones. An instruction from the fifteenth-century text *Illustrations for Designing Mountain, Water, and Hillside Field Landscapes* (*Senzui narabini yagyo no zu*) speaks of the "master rock" and its "attendant rocks." This relates to a general aesthetic rule—whether in gardening or painting or other forms of art and design—that there should be a visual hierarchy that allows the viewer to come naturally to the focal point of the composition. In the case of both the overall garden and the placement of individual stones,

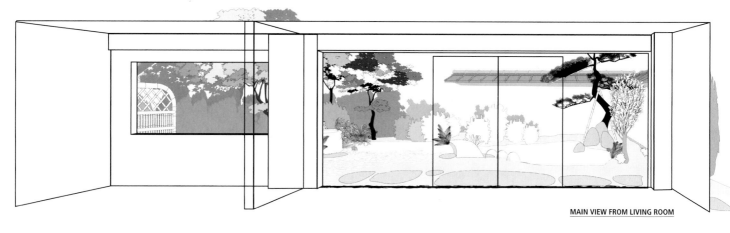

MAIN VIEW FROM LIVING ROOM

VIEW OF THE MEDIUM-SIZE GARDEN FROM CHAPTER 2, FRAMED BY DOOR AND WINDOW.

this means setting the main stone first, followed by the remaining stones in such a way that they seem to respond to the main stone. As regards this relationship, David A. Slawson, who published a translation of the above text, writes, "The Attendant Rocks take their compositional cues from the Master Rock. The Master Rock, however, looks not to other rocks but to the entire garden composition."

Another concept closely related to this is the so-called requesting mood of the stones. The eleventh-century *Sakuteiki* says, "You should first complete the placing of the principal rock having a distinct character, and then proceed to set each succeeding rock in compliance with the requesting mood of the principal rock." In other words, whatever the general requirements of the design, the specifics of how to set each particular stone can only be decided at the moment of the setting, and this is done, in part, by responding to what the stones themselves suggest.

This sense of master and attendant, as well as the idea of a requesting mood, is readily discernible in other creative arts. For example, many classic Western paintings on religious themes, including such works as Leonardo da Vinci's *Last Supper* and Raphael's *Transfiguration*, embrace the same concept. In Raphael's composition, the ascending Christ is placed higher in the composition than any other figure and is silhou-etted against a glowing light. All the other figures in the composition face each other or point back toward the ascending figure of Christ, while Christ faces the viewer and the overall composition. The eye moves easily around the composition, following unseen lines of force and visual relationship, and eventually set-tles once again on the main figure.

In setting stones in a Zen garden, two basic points will help determine where to begin and how to proceed:

First, consider the fact that, even though we are working with three-dimensional objects (stones) in a three-dimensional space (the garden), we will be viewing the garden from one side, or from specific locations along one side. This means we will be viewing the garden somewhat in the way we might view a painting or a stage. In addition, if we are viewing the garden primarily from inside a room of the house, the "frame" created by the architecture of the room is an important factor in the garden composition.

Second, consider the entire space—garden, enclosure, and sky—as the ground of your "canvas." Especially in the case of a stone-and-sand garden, which has a minimal number of dark objects on a light-colored ground, creating a composition that does not feel empty is a challenge. The natural tendency is to keep adding objects until the space feels full, but the greater challenge of "activating" the empty space on the canvas is one goal of our composition. Particularly important in this situation is the role of *ma*, a word in Japanese that refers to something which is "between" in both time and/or space. This "in-between" space, where there are no objects (known as background, "interstices," or negative-space in Western painting), is just as much a part of the visual effect as the objects themselves. The empty space is shaped by the objects, and the empty spaces are themselves important design elements in both physical terms (tension, proportion, and so on), and metaphorical terms (emotional, philosophical, etc.). To grasp this situation more easily, we'll make some simple sketches in black and white.

Take a piece of white paper and a felt-tip pen and draw a number of rectangles of the same size— about 3 inches (8 cm) wide by 2 inches (5 cm) tall. Within these frames we will sketch three simple stone-like shapes of different sizes in as many different arrangements as we can think of. What we are looking for is how best to energize the space around the stones, and how to emphasize the relationship between the stones and the space. Draw smaller shapes to indicate distance, and larger shapes to study a close-up

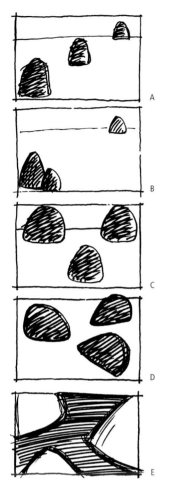

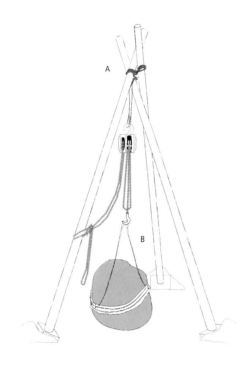

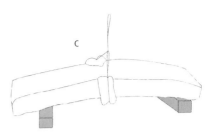

TYPICAL ARRANGEMENT OF TRIPOD AND CHAIN BLOCK FOR LIFTING AND PLACING STONES. **A**. Wire is tightly wrapped around each pole and then intertwined around the other poles to prevent slipping and to create a firm support for the chain-block. **B**. Wire is then looped around the stone such that the weight of the hanging stone pulls the loop tight. The total assembly is stabilized and the heaviest part of the stone is hanging directly below center. **c**. A horizontal stone, like this bridge stone, must be moved slowly, taking care not to swing or rock it.

◄ EXAMPLE OF FREE SKETCHING TO GAIN A SENSE OF THE RELATIONSHIP BETWEEN OBJECT AND GROUND. **A**. The sense of depth is lessened due to the regular spacing between the stones. **B**. Two stones grouped in the front against one in the back create a feeling of separation and distance. **c**. Three stones placed at regular intervals fail to activate the surrounding space. **D**. Three stones in a dynamic relation to each other energize the surrounding space. **E**. A close-up of the space between three stones, with the black/white relationship reversed to emphasize the shape of the space.

From ancient times, stone was imbued with taboos and myths and the power to bring good or evil to their owners. The shape and configuration of the stones in this garden seem to mark them as silent sentinels, watching over and protecting the occupants of the Kojimachi Kaikan Hotel in Tokyo. Garden by Masuno Shunmyo.

view of the space between the stones. Sketch freely and boldly. After you have accumulated twenty or more such sketches, it will start to become clear what it is that makes an arrangement quiet or energetic. With some practice it should become easier for you to shape and balance the empty space by adding, subtracting, or moving objects until the empty space is as interesting as the stones.

When it comes to the actual setting of the stones, you may require some help or even a truck with a crane suitable for small lifting jobs. If the stones are delivered from a quarry or supplier, try to have them unloaded close to where they will be used and placed on wooden supports near where you plan to set them in the ground. The stone can be lifted, lowered, or rotated with a tripod and chain block arrangement. After deciding the location and direction of each stone and how much of the stone will be above ground, draw a line on the stone with chalk where it should come level with the ground and dig a hole a little larger and deeper than the portion of the stone you intend to bury. Once the stone is lowered into the hole approximately as far as the line you have drawn, prop it up on some smaller stones, and have someone steady it in that position while you step back to take a look (it should still be attached to the chain block). Make adjustments by adding or removing smaller stones at the base to shift or raise one side or the other until you are satisfied with the placement. Continue to set the stones using your plan and your instincts, working from larger to smaller, and from farthest to nearest the viewing point.

If stones are to be set close to each other, make sure there is enough space underground to accommodate them, or dig a hole large enough to accommodate all of them at the same time. Be sure

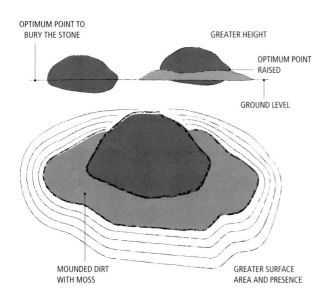

OPTIMUM POINT TO
BURY THE STONE

GREATER HEIGHT

OPTIMUM POINT
RAISED

GROUND LEVEL

MOUNDED DIRT
WITH MOSS

GREATER SURFACE
AREA AND PRESENCE

MOUNDING EARTH AROUND A STONE TO INCREASE ITS VOLUME
AND PRESENCE.

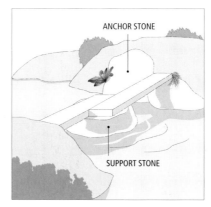

ANCHOR STONE

SUPPORT STONE

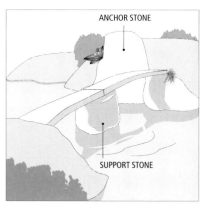

ANCHOR STONE

SUPPORT STONE

JOINTED STONE BRIDGES. Variations include from 1 to 3 flat, curved, or irregularly shaped sections. The height of one of the anchor stones is adjusted to balance the length, or "horizontality," of the bridge, while other, less visible stones, give support and stability.

to compact the earth before placing the stone. Once the position of a stone is set, refill the hole and pack the earth well under and around it. Finally, you can use a length of two-by-four to level the surface. Drag the wood back and forth across the refilled earth until it is level (a process similar to leveling wet cement).

Another possibility is to bury the stone at less than the optimum depth and heap the earth around the stone above the level of the gravel. This creates an area above the gravel for planting moss or other small plants and gives the stone an "island" setting as well as making it appear bigger than it is.

As you set the stones, keep in mind that your plan is a guideline, like a sketch for a painting. Remain flexible. Reevaluate the evolving composition as you set each new stone. Let a dialogue develop between you and what you are doing. Place each stone and ask, "What is happening now?" Keep a close watch on how your plan is developing as you implement it and respond to any major or subtle changes, or images you note. Remember that the layout and the actual implementation are two different things. Pay special attention to the space around the stones and constantly evaluate the relation to the overall space of the garden. If you respond to what you actually see rather than what you thought you would see, your next move will always be right—even if it is not the move you were planning. For example, as the garden takes shape, you might feel the need for a different or an additional stone to respond to the developing composition. It is best therefore to keep a few extra stones on hand.

ADDITIONAL USES OF STONE

Stone is used in a variety of ways other than as the main objects or "bones" of the garden. One such use is as a bridge over a real or dry stream, or to an island located in a real or dry pond. Some are purely decorative or symbolic; others are intended to be actually used. A stone to be used as a bridge is generally thick, long, smooth on top, and flat or slightly arched. Such stones need to be well secured at both ends with dirt, smaller stones, or cement, if necessary. When more than one stone is employed, they are often arranged to create a staggered joint at the center that breaks up the strict geometry. The center joint will often rest on a large natural stone, most of which for the sake of stability will be submerged in the pond and the clay beneath it, and it may be rough in its finish to conform with the naturalness of the setting.

Other common uses of stone in the Japanese garden are as stepping stones (*tobi ishi*) and walkways (*nobedan* or *tatami ishi*); retaining walls (*ishigaki*); steps (*ishidan*); as boundaries to create and support the banks of ponds (*gogan seki*); as the edge of a stream and/or to direct its flow; in waterfalls (*taki*); for waterbasins (*tsukubai* and *chozubachi*); and in stone lanterns (*ishidoro*).

This massive mountain of stone and trees in a park in Kansai Science City is entirely manmade, composed of some five hundred stones weighing in at twenty to seventy tons each.

TYPES OF STONE

In this book I use the words "rock" and "stone" almost interchangeably. Names of stones used in this book may differ from names used in your area. Since names and meaning often vary from region to region, when ordering material it is advisable to first obtain a sample or at least a photograph of the material.

The geological classification of stone includes broad categories such as igneous, metamorphic, and sedimentary. All types are used in the garden, but igneous stone is probably the most common, with granite being the most common of that group. The availability of materials in the following basic list varies by country and region. As mentioned above, searching for local stone or digging at the site itself should not be ignored. If that produces no results, begin searching at local suppliers.

Granite

In Japan, *mikage ishi* (granite) is used widely in both modern construction and traditional gardens. Although mostly light to dark grays are used in the garden, a wide range of colors are available. Granite is relatively hard but easily shaped into stone basins, lanterns, decorative pagodas, and other symbolic Buddhist objects such as "five-wheel pagodas" (*gorinto*) and a popular bodhisattva (*jizo*). It is used extensively for stepping stones, walkways, and most other garden elements.

Blue Stone

This is *ao ishi* in Japanese. It is a chlorite schist and actually more grayish blue-green than blue. It contains white striations that give it a distinct and highly prized marbling. As a metamorphic stone, the surface often looks folded and layered, giving a single stone a mountainlike image. In its cut and processed form, it finds use as floor surfacing in Japanese hot-spring baths, since, even when wet, it has a dry, nonslippery quality and changes color drastically from a soft grayish blue-green when dry to a deep sea-green when wet. Schist appears in a fairly wide range of colors, from a pale gray-green to a purplish gray. It is not the same as California blue schist, which is sodium-rich and bluer.

Volcanic Rock

There are a number of types of volcanic rock, with colors ranging from gray to black and light to dark brown,

This apartment house plaza by landscape architect Inoue Yoji and sculptor Yagi Yoshio explores the intimate connection between garden art as embodied in stone-and-sand gardens, and modern landscape architecture and sculpture. Inoue uses undifferentiated white granite as a stark contrasting base for Yagi's naturalistic forms, stressing the increasing ambiguity in our world about the meaning of natural and man-made.

and textures ranging from dense to highly pockmarked. Those with abundant gas bubble cavities are seldom used, but andesite rock with a fine grain is widely employed. Andesite is relatively hard and not unlike granite in appearance.

Marble

Marble (*dairiseki*) was not traditionally used in Japanese gardens, and there are few native deposits, although it is often imported for the construction industry. Sculptors use the material extensively and the building of more public plazas has brought both garden designers and landscape architects into contact with it. It has been occasionally and successfully used in modern gardens by Japanese-American sculptor Isamu Noguchi, well-known garden designer Suzuki Shodo, and others—but not in traditional-style gardens. However, its availability, wide range of colors and textures, and workability make it an interesting option in modern interpretations.

Volcanic Tuff

Because this material, called "*ooya ishi*," is pockmarked and crumbles with time, it is considered unsuitable for stone arrangements. However, due to its relative cheapness, availability, and interesting surface texture and color (most often beige with scattered rusty-colored iron deposits), this material is often used for walls and paving in polished and unpolished form. This stone was employed extensively by Frank Lloyd Wright in the old Imperial Hotel in Tokyo. It is becoming increasingly difficult to mine in Japan and availability has decreased.

Slate

Widely available and extensively used in gardens and houses, slate is the lowest-grade metamorphic stone and is usually found in shades of black and rust-brown. Its natural tendency to split off into flat sections makes it ideal for paving.

Pumice

This is occasionally found in Japanese gardens where lightweight stone is desirable, such as roofs, terraces, and verandas. In these locations, it may need to be protected from strong winds by tall barriers, or placed where it will not easily be disturbed.

A spiral pattern composed of white and tan gravel and large natural stones is used to express the idea of spouting energy and an expanding future in this dry garden by Masuno Shunmyo.

Cobblestones

Cobblestones (*tama ishi* and *gorota*) are generally distinguished by their size—between 2 and 14 inches (5 and 30 cm)—and are used for paving, areas around ponds, stream and pond beds, and walls. When used as paving, the round stones are always set in dry mortar, sand, or cement. Most cobblestones are of granite and are generally in grays and browns.

Pebbles

Pebbles (*kuri ishi*) are usually between 1 and 2 inches (2 and 5 cm) in diameter. The rounded and semipolished types are used as edging material where rain runoff occurs around stone and sand gardens, as well as in combination with stone waterbasins to cover and disguise drainage areas. For this purpose, jet-black and other colors, including blues, reds, and pure white are often employed.

Sand and Gravel

The word *suna* is used interchangeably in Japanese to mean "gravel" and "sand," which may account for some confusion in calling a *kare sansui* a "sand garden." The material referred to as "sand" is usually gravel that, in the context of the garden, lends a sandlike effect. A gravel of naturally decomposed or processed granite measuring from 1/16 to 5/8 of an inch (2 to 15 mm) in diameter is most common and ranges in color from dull white to dark gray and tan.

The use of light-colored granite-based gravel as a surface material has a very long history in Japan. In ancient times, whitish gravel was spread on the sacred grounds of Shinto shrines as a ritual act of purification. Later, this role was extended to include the area in front of the main hall of the emperor's palace, which was also sacred since the emperor was revered as a direct descendant of the gods. Thereafter, symbolic use was melded to the practical application of surfacing large, flat expanses for use in ceremonial functions. It is still used today in this capacity as an inexpensive surfacing 1 to 2 inches (2.5 to 5 cm) deep over large areas leading to temples, shrines, and castles, and it makes a distinct crunching sound when trodden on. Gravel degrades over time and needs "topping up" to preserve its pristine appearance. This is said to be one purpose of the cone-shaped mounds of gravel seen in some temples. When special guests are due to visit, fresh gravel from the mounds is spread out to renew the whiteness of the garden.

It was during the fifteenth century that a leap of thinking cast sand in the abstract role of representing water. Whether the direct result of Zen or some other influence, this supernatural image has survived the centuries to resonate deeply in our modern consciousness.

GRAVEL AND PEBBLES. The photographs on this page show a wide variety of stone colors sizes, shapes, and types. From the top right, colors range from black to gray, red, tan, and white. Sizes run from 1/16 inch (2 mm) for gravel, to 1 1/2 inches (40 mm) for large pebbles. Shapes are jagged for gravel and rounded for polished to semipolished pebbles. Almost any type of stone is used, including marble. General characteristics to consider are the weight of the stone, the degree of color change and surface gloss when wet, and hardness.

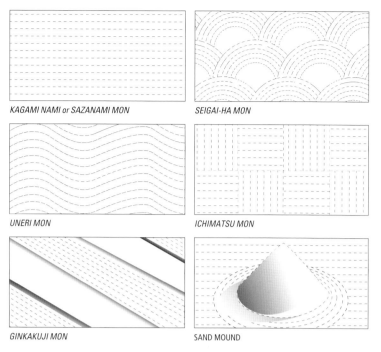

KAGAMI NAMI or SAZANAMI MON

SEIGAI-HA MON

UNERI MON

ICHIMATSU MON

GINKAKUJI MON

SAND MOUND

EXAMPLES OF SAND PATTERNS. Patterns (*samon*) generally allude to water but exceptions almost exceed the rule. The basic idea of raking is cleanliness and to impart a sense of both constancy and renewal.

RAKING A CHECKERBOARD PATTERN. A gardener at Zenrinji temple in Kyoto creates a checkerboard pattern (*ichimatsu*) on a raised sand mound by pressing the rake into the gravel and raking lightly toward his body as he pulls the rake up, then pressing it down again at a fixed interval and repeating the process.

LAYING GRAVEL AND SAND AND DESIGNING PATTERNS

A layer of compacted clay and gravel is generally spread under the gravel to prevent it being soiled by dirt churned up from beneath and to retard the growth of weeds. The gravel is generally raked into patterns, most commonly waves, to symbolize water. As the practice evolved, various patterns were created. For example, at the Honenin temple in Kyoto, named after the founder of the Jodo sect of Buddhism, there are two rectangular sand mounds about 10 to 12 inches (25 to 30 cm) in height. The top surface of each is raked into a pattern—organic forms, swirls, and so on—that is changed every few weeks by the resident monks. Sand patterns are an area of garden-making with very little specific instruction. New patterns are constantly created and are usually a reaction to a specific garden design. At a minimum, a 12-inch- (30-cm-) wide band around stones and the edge of the garden is raked, and the rest left untouched.

Direct sunlight reflected from large areas of sand can be extremely glaring and hard on the eyes. The reflected light and heat can wither plants or burn the fine needles of trees such as the black pine. As a result, plantings and trees that are surrounded by sand must be selected and maintained with care.

On the other hand, in interior or small courtyard gardens or other areas that receive little direct light, sand gardens are a good way to brighten up the area and bring reflected light indoors. The combination of stone lantern, stone waterbasin, and small plantings on a gravel base is the typical form of the enclosed Kyoto-style courtyard garden. As a general rule of thumb, the smaller the space, the smaller the size of gravel that should be used. If the area is fully protected from the wind, even a fine sand may be suitable, although fine sand is rarely used outdoors.

Rakes

Rakes for creating patterns in the sand are generally constructed from a flat wooden board cut in a deep sawtooth pattern. Depending on the pitch of the teeth, the raked waves will be wider or narrower. Another type of rake utilizes a length of two-by-four. Holes are drilled at regular intervals on one side and pegs are inserted, then a handle is inserted on the back side in another hole. Again the pitch of the pegs will determine the width of the waves. Several rakes of different sizes are likely to be employed in one garden. Narrow rakes, sometimes without handles, are used for detail work around stones or for tight turns and smaller patterns. Wider rakes are used on long, straight expanses. Overall width should be limited to about 25 inches (64 cm) or it will become impossible to drag.

Having looked at some of the components, materials, and methods of placing stones in the garden, we will now look at one specific instance of stone setting.

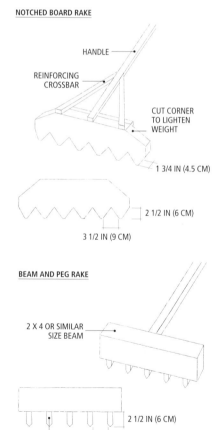

NOTCHED BOARD RAKE

HANDLE

REINFORCING CROSSBAR

CUT CORNER TO LIGHTEN WEIGHT

1 3/4 IN (4.5 CM)

2 1/2 IN (6 CM)

3 1/2 IN (9 CM)

BEAM AND PEG RAKE

2 X 4 OR SIMILAR SIZE BEAM

2 1/2 IN (6 CM)

SQUARE PEGS CUT AT A 45° ANGLE

3 1/2 IN (9 CM)

ROUND PEGS

EXAMPLE OF RAKE CONSTRUCTION. The depth and pitch of the rake teeth is variable. Find the right balance through trial and error using notched plywood boards, without a handle, before final construction.

The building's steel columns "stand-in" for stones in this *kare sansui* installation by architect Kori Yumi. The concentric rings of raked gravel seem to emanate from the poles like waves generated by a stone tossed in still waters.

The sharpness and planiform nature of the massive stones in this dry garden by Masuno Shunmyo mark it clearly as a work of the modern era. Though quarried stone defies the tradition of using only naturally occurring and worn stone, both environmental necessity and modern aesthetics increasingly call for the use of quarried and fashioned stone. Very large stones, arrayed in a confined space—used successfully by designer Suzuki Shodo and others—is another innovation of the twentieth century. In some measure this may reflect a desire to experience the rough power of nature in the otherwise overly formal and geometric confines of the urban environment.

ARRANGING A "DRY WATERFALL"
by Masuno Shunmyo

Both actual waterfalls and dry waterfalls—that is, a stone configuration designed to represent a waterfall—are an important element of the Japanese garden. Actual waterfalls may be found in gardens in other parts of the world, but dry waterfalls are unique to Japan, largely due to the influence of Zen. With this in mind, I will illustrate one basic setting.

MASUNO SHUNMYO Is the abbot of Kenkoji, a Zen temple of the Soto sect, located in Yokohama. He studied forestry at Tamagawa University and established Japan Landscape Consultants with his younger brother, Yoshihiko, in 1982. He has a number of major gardens to his credit both in Japan and in Canada, Scotland, Germany, and, most recently, Norway, where his design was chosen by competition. His credits in Japan include the garden of the Canadian Embassy and the Cerulean Tower Tokyu Hotel, both in Tokyo.

—— *"A garden based on plantings is subject to great change over time, whereas a garden of stone may endure unchanged. In this respect, the original work and intentions of the designer are more lasting, along with the strengths and weaknesses of the design. Plantings can be shaped and changed over time and will tend to create a pleasant atmosphere even if unattended. Once set, the stone is there forever. Therefore, the placement of the stone must be precise. In the modern world, the meaning of a garden is often reduced to nothing more than a buffer between buildings. The nature of building today is such that the exterior is often completely divorced from the interior environment. Homes and public buildings no longer open out to exterior spaces in the manner of the traditional Japanese structure. Especially since the Meiji period (1868–1912) in Japan, glass and solid-wall construction imported from the West has altered the living style. With the increasing creation of artificial atmospheres today, this separation of interior from exterior has become complete, but I believe unity can be reasserted through the design of the garden. In order to achieve this, the expression of modern architecture in glass, steel, and concrete can be positively met with traditional Japanese aesthetics, values, and traditional skills, and the construction of the garden in stone."*

1. The basic waterfall is composed of three stones: the *Fudo seki*, the waterfall, or "mirror," stone (*mizu ochi ishi* or *kagami ishi*), and the big stone (*oya ishi*). The *Fudo seki* is the largest of the three and is set first.

2. The *Fudo seki* is likened to Fudo-myoo (a fierce incarnation of the cosmic Buddha from Esoteric Buddhism), whose strength and powerful stance can be felt in a dynamic waterfall. To project a stronger image, the stone should be set leaning slightly inward (to the left).

3. Set the shorter, flatter mirror stone next to and slightly behind the *Fudo seki*. This will lean slightly forward and rest against the *Fudo seki*. It may need to be propped up with a wooden post and secured with a rope to the *Fudo seki* until the next stone is set in place.

4. The *oya ishi* is smaller than the *Fudo seki* and set to the left and slightly in front of the mirror stone. It leans toward the right, but not at the same angle as the *Fudo seki* or the arrangement will look symmetrical and artificial. When finished, all three stones should look as if they are locked together.

5. After these three stones are set, begin placing smaller stones extending from the *oya ishi* and *Fudo seki* to form a circular pattern that is closed with a very low stone that echoes the shape of the mirror stone. In actual waterfalls, the circle of stones collects the fallen water, which then overflows and falls again from the smaller mirror stone.

6. Finally, a "wave-dividing" stone (*mizu-wake ishi*) is placed slightly off-center and "looking" toward the mirror stone. Another stone, the "water-hitting" stone (*mizu-tataki ishi*) in the shape of a carp trying to get upstream (*rigyo seki*), is often placed at the base of the mirror stone.

7. After the stones are placed, gravel is laid and raked around the water-dividing stone, with some spilling past the lower mirror stone.

1–2 *FUDO-SEKI* STONE, LEANING INWARD

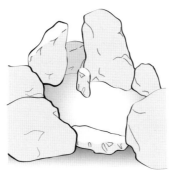

3 THE MIRROR STONE, PROPPED AND TIED

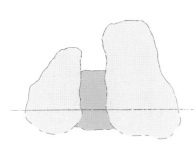

4 THE *OYA ISHI* STONE COMPLETES THIS VITAL TRIO

5–6 FINISHED DRY WATERFALL

A more panoramic view of the dry waterfall in combination with a dry pond, stone bridge, and island.

CHAPTER 4

WATER AND RELATED GARDEN FIXTURES

A beautifully crafted pond and garden by Aoki Yasujiro wraps around this ultra-modern, glass-wall tea house by architect Kihara Chitoshi. The flowing water freshens the air and offers the soothing sound of water running over pebbles. Not normally a part of tea gardens, the pond and building give a sense of what the fishing pavilion in the *shinden*-style garden (see page 9) must have been like.

Ever since man began to explore the universe, we have come to understand that the existence of water equals the existence of life. Even without such exploration, the connection is instinctively understood. No wonder, then, that when we think of a garden in terms of relaxation, refreshment, and rejuvenation, we often think of water.

In Japan, a country with a high annual rainfall as well as wet rice cultivation, water plays a central role in the lives of the people. Ethnologist Yanagida Kunio noted that farmers dug ponds on their land because "the sight and sound of flowing water calmed their minds [with the assurance of good crops]."

Not only ponds but the streams that fed them have been important features of the Japanese garden since ancient times. The fifteenth-century text on garden-making referred to in the last chapter states, "Mountains [piled-up earth], water, and stones are like the three legs of a tripod—if even one is missing there can be no garden."

In this chapter we will highlight some of the most important symbolic meanings, design features, and construction considerations of ponds, streams, waterfalls, and various fixtures used in Japanese gardens.

POND DESIGN

A pond (*ike*) with an island was probably the original form of the Japanese garden. It is thought that palaces in antiquity may have been built on the islands and then, from about the seventh or eighth century, moved adjacent to the pond. In those early times, newly imported Chinese geomancy dictated that the most auspicious location for a building had a pond on the south side and a river on the east flowing from the north-east. Even after the palace location was moved, the pond still contained one or more islands and was used for boating in Chinese-style dragon and phoenix-head boats.

As the centuries passed, the size of estates shrank considerably and the size of the pond followed accordingly. Today, ponds are still found on large estates, although the dragon boats are long gone. The largest ponds, however, are located in the old *daimyo* stroll gardens that have become public parks, and on the grounds of the largest Buddhist temples.

Imagery used in pond design remains from those ancient times and is related primarily to Chinese influence (the myth of Horai, or the "Island of Eternal Youth"), symbolic abstractions of Chinese characters

Architect Kishi Warou confines the pond and brings it right up to the house in this home located in Wakayama, central Japan. The experience of looking from the window down into water is perhaps more akin to that of a boat on a placid bay than to a building on solid ground.

A cascading pond/waterfall in the large courtyard of this apartment complex in Tokyo is mingled with lush ground cover and tall trees to create an oasis in the.heart of the city. As if that were not enough, designer Inoue Yoji has added a water fogger, creating a dreamlike, as well as refreshing, atmosphere.

for heart (*kokoro* or *shin*) or water (*mizu*), Buddhist influence (especially the Western Paradise image), and native Japanese imagery based primarily on references to natural waterscapes (of ocean, pond, and river), and island scenes.

For most people today, the symbolism is secondary to considerations of use, size, construction problems, costs, and maintenance. These factors will probably play a greater role in the style and shape of your pond and whether it contains such features as islands, bridges, and ornamental Japanese carp (*koi*). Obviously, each type has its specific details and problems to consider. Very large ponds require contractors, permits, extensive maintenance, and the attendant costs. Besides the care involved in maintaining the fish, construction of a *koi* pond requires a careful selection of nontoxic materials, adequate filtration and antibacterial safeguards, water temperature control, and so on. However, small- to medium-size ponds are quite within the range of the average home owner.

In terms of the traditional appearance of the pond in Japanese gardens, whether symbolic or otherwise, the guiding principle is organic, irregular, and asymmetrical composition. The boundaries or edges of the pond should blend gracefully with the surrounding landscape and seem to have developed as a natural consequence of the landscape around it. The application of landscape "themes," such as "wave-swept beach" or "rocky-shore style," is meant to guide the designer and help decide both the shape and the use of materials. For example, a wave-swept beach brings to mind a gently sloping shore, with scattered, well-worn pebbles. Perhaps an old twisted pine tree, which seems to have weathered many seasons of sun, wind, and rain, stands proudly nearby. The water level is high and calmly envelopes the sloping bank. A rocky shore calls to mind a jagged coast, with many rocky inlets and outcrops, and a rock face that plunges steeply into the low level of water. Here, the same twisted pines are smaller, perhaps greater in number, and leaning over the edge of powerful stones that seem to be their protectors. In this way, materials and shapes are suggested, and the design process begins by going to such places, taking pictures, collecting books, and sketching out ideas.

In the same way, when constructing the pond, the placement of materials such as stones, plants, and other elements should adhere to the spirit of naturalism and be consistent with the design of the garden. For example, around the edge of a pond, stones of similar shape and size placed at regular intervals would look unnatural, so this arrangement should be avoided. Notice that in our large-scale layout in Chapter 2 (page 28), we varied the pond edge by creating a kind of promontory jutting out toward the center of the pond. This is a fairly common device. The rocky promontory creates a strategic location for a lantern, which itself becomes a key feature of the garden. The bank on either side of the promontory is shallow and paved with a display of cobblestones that seem to emerge gradually from the water. Overall, the height of the pond edge is low in relation to the water level, in keeping with the image of a serene mountain lake. The

A vast pool of water within a strictly geometric plaza in front of the Shinano Museum in Nagano Prefecture is made to echo natural wetlands through architect Taniguchi Yoshio's seemingly casual addition of piled cobblestones. This device recalls the tradition of creating cobblestone peninsulas in garden ponds, the most famous of which is located in the garden of Katsura Imperial Villa in Kyoto.

near bank slopes gently up from the water to the ground level of the garden, and the far bank uses clusters of medium and small stones, with earth piled up behind them, interspersed with ferns, rushes, and wild-flowers, in total creating a soft but solid impression.

Having reviewed traditional Japanese principles, it should also be mentioned that, in modern garden design, geometric or other obviously man-made shapes are being employed increasingly. When incorporating such ponds, however, the possibility of the final appearance being in harmony with the spirit of naturalism and repose will be greater if traditional design principles are absorbed first, then filtered through your own modern experience and sensibilities.

POND CONSTRUCTION

Pond construction variables are as numerous as the sizes, purposes, and locations of the ponds themselves. One aspect is the totally different circumstances of the traditional and modern garden in relation to water sources and drainage. Whereas natural sources of water were once the norm, it is probable that ponds today will be fed by a chlorinated, fluorinated, and expensive city-water supply. It is also most likely that drainage and construction will be subject to local regulations. For home owners familiar with the construction and maintenance of swimming pools, this may sound familiar; for others it may seem daunting.

Simple setups may require no more than a waterproof tub inserted in a hole in the ground, filled with water from a garden hose and a drain connection or a submersible pump leading to an external drain. Larger ponds may require a Butyl rubber liner, and reinforced concrete with a recirculation pump, water-level detecting float, filtration system, skimmers, and purifiers.

The traditional Japanese pond calls for multiple layers of small cobblestones (with diameters of between 4 and 6 inches; 10 and 15 cm) and compacted clay, the best of which is said to come from the bottom of rice fields that have been in use for a long time. These days, mortar with sealer over reinforced concrete, and/or rubber liners are more common inside and outside Japan, but they are not without problems.

A liner, placed in a shallow, 1- to 2-foot deep hole with gently sloping sides, is perhaps the simplest method for a small reflecting pond. Care needs to be exercised to avoid puncturing the liner, especially when stones are placed over the edge to hide and anchor the liner. Oxygenating plants and small fish can be added to keep the water reasonably clean without any filters or pumps. Water can be drained from time to time with a small exterior or submersible pump. The key is to skillfully model the edge and avoid an even ring of stone. Consider burying some of the stones anchoring the liner with soil and creating a grass-covered edge.

While simple reflection ponds need not be deep, ponds for *koi* may need to be as deep as 5 to 6 feet (150 to 180 cm) in cold-weather climates where freezing water is a problem. Keep in mind that greater size and depth increase the volume of water, which in turn affects every aspect of construction as well as maintenance cost. A tank for capturing rainwater from gutters can be a clean and totally free alternative source of pond water if space is available.

When it comes to emptying the pond, basically two choices are available: bottom drains or pumps. Drains are recommended, especially for larger or deeper ponds. Pumps may be submersible or located in a well adjacent to the pond. Finally, with any type of pond, even a shallow one, safety is a consideration—especially if young children will be playing in the garden.

STREAMS

In many respects streams (*nagare*) have traditionally been as important a feature of the garden as ponds. In Japan, where space considerations often dictate design imperatives, streams sometimes replace ponds entirely as the main water feature of a garden. In a garden that lacks physical depth, for example, a winding stream is similar in effect to a winding road in a painting—it creates the illusion of depth. Closely related to this is the visual illusion that the stream narrows toward its source and widens downstream. This effect can be achieved by exaggeratedly narrowing the far end and widening the near end of the stream. Here again the analogy of the road disappearing into the distance applies.

The volume and speed of the water that flows in the stream depends on a large number of factors. Primary among these is the image you want to project. As with ponds, a mountain river conjures an image of a rushing, rocky stream, whereas a pastoral image demands a trickling, winding stream lined with wild flowers and reeds.

As with ponds, the stream needs to be tightly sealed against leakage, for example, with mortar-and-sealer or compacted clay and stone. When water is running in a winding stream, there may be erosion to the outer bank of each curve or silt build-up on the inner bank. Erosion is usually handled with the strategic placement of stones, plants, or compacted clay. Silt build-up needs to be cleaned away periodically. The placement of stones in the stream is particularly important for the overall naturalism of the effect. In nature, the flow of water hitting a stone and being redirected by it helps define the shape of the stream.

The sound of the water in a stream is one of its greatest charms. Such devices as small cascades over a stone ledge, stones placed in the middle of the stream for water to run against and around, and narrowing the stream between stones to accelerate the water flow and create turbulence can combine to produce just the right level of sound. Where only a small amount of water is available, large gravel embedded in the mortar stream-bed promotes a gentle trickling sound.

This vast and multistepped "cloth falls" (*nuno ochi*) is entirely man-made, stunning visitors to the Kansai Science City park with a *tour de force* of stone setting. The park contains excellent examples of smaller waterfalls in a combination nature park–stroll garden.

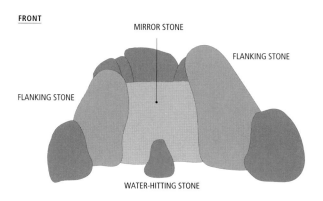

FRONT

MIRROR STONE

FLANKING STONE

FLANKING STONE

WATER-HITTING STONE

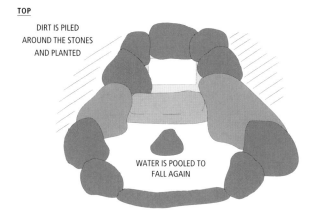

TOP

DIRT IS PILED
AROUND THE STONES
AND PLANTED

WATER IS POOLED TO
FALL AGAIN

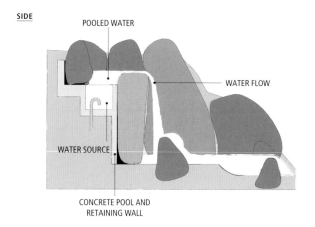

SIDE

POOLED WATER

WATER FLOW

WATER SOURCE

CONCRETE POOL AND
RETAINING WALL

SIDE

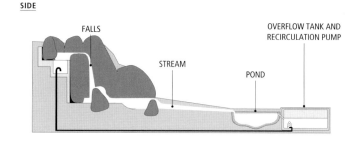

FALLS

STREAM

POND

OVERFLOW TANK AND
RECIRCULATION PUMP

WATERFALLS

The waterfall (*taki*) plays a major role in traditional gardens. In a mountainous country such as Japan, the high mountain waterfall has always been one of the most moving natural scenes. In the native Shinto belief, waterfalls are often regarded as the dwelling place of gods, and the image of the mountain monk standing under an ice-cold barrage of a waterfall represents a well-known ancient ascetic pursuit that is still practiced today.

The art of making a proper waterfall requires long study, and its construction is perhaps the most difficult aspect of water use in the garden. This is where the stonework in a garden is often at its finest and most complex. At a minimum, waterfalls require three stones: the central stone, usually referred to as the "mirror" stone, which creates a ledge over which the water will fall, and one stone on either side of the mirror stone. These flanking stones are generally taller than the mirror stone and serve to direct the flow of water over its edge. A pool is created behind the lip of the mirror stone in order to collect the water before it falls and to keep the flow consistant across the lip of the falls. The flanking stones may be somewhat sharp or jagged, but the mirror stone should be rounded enough to look worn down by the continuously falling water.

Smaller stones are then added to the front and sides of the flanking stones to create a mountainlike effect and a gradual transition to ground level. A "water-hitting" stone is often added at the base of the fall so that the falling water strikes it, creating more sound, spray, and visual interest. The classic example of this type is the "carp" stone mentioned in the instructions on making a dry waterfall at the end of Chapter 3. In addition, one or more steps can be added before the stream reaches the lower level of the pond. By changing the angle of the steps or shifting them sideways, each step creates a smaller cascade that can also be used to redirect the stream in a natural-looking way.

One important consideration is in getting air to mix with the falling water to produce the highly visible "white water" indicative of a natural falls. This is accomplished with one or more "V" shaped depressions in the top of the mirror stone.

BASIC COMPONENTS OF A WATERFALL. One point of caution when using re-circulation pumps involves the size of the pump reservoir. When the pump is turned off for the night, all the water in the falls and the stream flows into the pond, which then overflows into the reservoir. Therefore the capacity of the reservoir should be equal to or greater than all the water in the system. If the waterline in the reservoir falls below the pump line, the pump will quickly overheat.

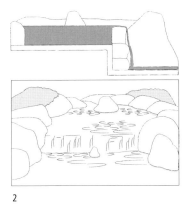

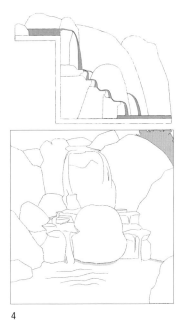

1

2

3

4

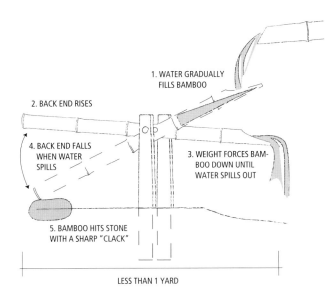

WATERFALL TYPES.

1. The "stepped falls" (*dan-ochi*) is like a series of steps, whereby falling water is pooled and falls again, each step being turned or shifted left or right, until the water reaches the level of the pond.

2. The "cloth falls" (*nuno-ochi*) is like a small Niagara in that it is broad and flat, without any large flanking stones, and the water drops evenly in a "curtain" effect. This type is generally not very tall and requires a rather straight, natural or processed mirror stone to produce the right effect.

3. The "ribbon" or "thread falls" (*ito-ochi*) is so-called because the water falls in a singular strand, focused by a depression or notch in the mirror stone. This type of fall needs a little height and should make a good bit of splash and spray when it hits one or more stones placed in its falling path or at its base.

4. The thread falls is actually one type of a group of "separated falls" (*hanare-ochi*) that depend on the water falling away from the mirror stone and dropping through the air, rather than running down the surface of other stones—as in the stepped falls and cloth falls styles. This is accomplished by setting the mirror stone to lean slightly forward, or using a mirror stone shaped somewhat like the spout of a tea kettle, both of which force the water to arch away from the stone as it falls.

Another prime consideration is the height and width of the falls. More specifically, it is the proportion between height and width that affects the final appearance of the falls. If the waterfall is tall, the flanking stones close together, and the mirror stone narrow and set back, the effect is reminiscent of a deep-forest, mountain waterfall. If the falls are shorter, with the flanking stones set wide apart, the effect sugests a waterfall at the end of a great river. It is generally necessary to start from a height above eye level in order to disguise the fact that the water is not running from an actual stream. In addition, a craggy pine or juniper, set at a precipitous angle, is often used to partially obscure the view of the falls and add depth. The height of the falls also relates to such things as the number of cascades before the water reaches pond level, or whether there will be one single drop.

While a waterfall is built out of stone, it may need a cement retaining structure to support the stone, and piled-up earth to help create a natural-looking environment around the waterfall. Earth is also added between the rocks so that plantings can complete the scene.

PRODUCING SOUND WITH WATER

In addition to the sounds created by streams and waterfalls, another classical sound generated by a water feature known as the "deer scare" (*shishi odoshi*), is a sharp clack that was originally used near fields to prevent crops being damaged by wild deer, boar, and other animals. Take a length of bamboo about 1 yard long and at least 4 inches (10 cm) in diameter and mount it between two upright wooden posts. Use a narrow dowel to pass through the posts and the bamboo to form a pivot. The posts should be about 20 inches (50 cm) in height and stuck directly into the ground. The bamboo is mounted off center so that the long side naturally drops to the ground. The short end is cut at a steep angle to form an upward-facing scoop that collects water from a pipe or some other source. As the scoop fills with water, the weight causes the short side to fall slowly (raising the long end) until it passes the level point and the collected water spills out of the scoop. The sudden emptying causes the long end to fall back to its natural position. Place a stone at the point where the long end strikes the ground and adjust the height until a sharp clap results when the bamboo strikes the stone. The time it takes to fill the short end becomes the interval between claps. In other words, the shorter the filling time the more frequent the claps. A prolonged filling time and lengthy interval between claps is recommended.

1. WATER GRADUALLY FILLS BAMBOO

2. BACK END RISES

4. BACK END FALLS WHEN WATER SPILLS

3. WEIGHT FORCES BAMBOO DOWN UNTIL WATER SPILLS OUT

5. BAMBOO HITS STONE WITH A SHARP "CLACK"

LESS THAN 1 YARD

CONSTRUCTION OF A "DEER-SCARE."

A classic waterbasin (*tsukubai*) is rendered here in a tea garden in Tokyo by garden designer Yasumoro Sadao.

STONE WATERBASINS

Water also plays a central role in both Shinto and Buddhist purification ceremonies. It is for the ritual cleaning of hands and mouth that a waterbasin and dippers made of cedar, cypress, or bamboo are found in front of almost every Buddhist temple and Shinto shrine. The tea ceremony incorporated this ritual in the stone waterbasin (*tsukubai* or *chozubachi*), which has been a feature of every tea garden since the sixteenth century.

The difference between the *tsukubai* and the *chozubachi* is that the *chozubachi* is placed higher to afford ease of access while standing, or is placed within reach from a room of the house or an exterior deck. It was in the tea garden that the waterbasin was first placed close to the ground so that a person would need to bow in a gesture of humility when using it. This type is called a *tsukubai* ("crouching waterbasin").

It is not difficult to construct a *tsukubai*. The main difference between it and an ordinary sink is that the *tsukubai* basin has no drain and no faucet. Instead, excess water is allowed to flow over the edge of the basin to a drain concealed near the base. This drain is concealed by an arrangement of gravel and pebbles on which the waterbasin is placed. Water is either collected from rain, brought from another source, or piped into the basin. The typical piping method involves an external spigot with a bamboo spout (*kakehi*), through which the water flows into the basin. Any metal or plastic fittings are concealed

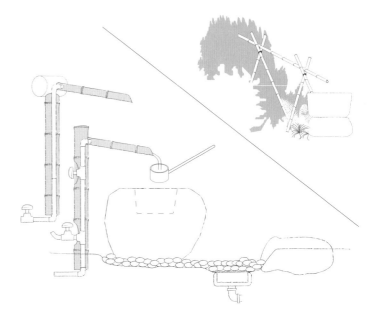

CONSTRUCTION OF A WATERBASIN AND WATER SPOUT. Several variations are shown in these illustrations. The lower drawing shows two types of water spout: one using bamboo only, one using a block of wood (either square or round) at the joint. The spout end can be cut in a number of ways but should not be cut at too sharp an angle. Finally, while dimensions for the proper height of the water spout in relation to the basin will vary, a simple rule of thumb is that the space between the two should comfortably accommodate the water ladle being placed in the path of the falling water without touching the water in the basin. In addition, the spout should be positioned so that the water falls in the center of the basin. *Top insert*: Design for a waterspout coming from a remote location and supported by bamboo struts.

A modern rendition of the *tsukubai* done in stainless steel and polished granite by architect Izue Kan for a tea house and garden (also designed by him) on the roof of a community center in Hyogo Prefecture, near Kobe.

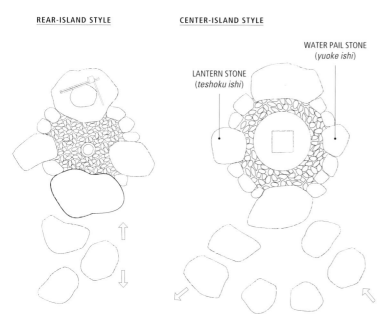

REAR-ISLAND STYLE   **CENTER-ISLAND STYLE**

WATER PAIL STONE
(*yuoke ishi*)

LANTERN STONE
(*teshoku ishi*)

WATERBASIN ARRANGEMENTS. Both the rear- and center-island styles should be arranged in a circular form which can be constructed of stone or compacted clay (*doma*). The heights of the surrounding stones should vary with the *teshoku* and *yuoke* stones being higher than the others but not equal in height. In the center-island style, the stone at the rear is usually the tallest.

within a length of bamboo channel, sometimes topped with a wooden block. Sometimes this *kakehi* is quite long, extending from a water source that is far away and concealed. In this case, the *kakehi* is supported by bamboo braces, which are planted in the ground and tied in an X shape with black hemp rope.

The word *tsukubai* includes the basin and the arrangement of stones around it, of which there are basically two types: the "center style" (*nakabachi*) and the "far edge style" (*mukaibachi*). As the names imply, in the first case the basin is placed in the center of a "sea" of pebbles, surrounded by stones higher and lower in height than itself. This may also include a stone on which to place a pail of hot water in winter (*yuoke ishi*) and one on which to stand a light (*teshoku ishi*). Of the surrounding stones, the one directly in front of the basin is flat and a little larger than the others, and this is where a person stands when reaching for the water. In the second case the basin is placed at the rear of the circle of stones, while the stone to stand on is again the front stone (making the water a little farther away). A dipper (*hishaku*) made of cedar, cypress, or bamboo is placed on the basin.

The variety in the sizes and shapes of waterbasins is inexhaustible. This is one place in the garden in which square or round shapes are often employed, and it is also where the practice of using an object in a new context (*mitate*) is most common. Thus, everything from the bases of stone lanterns to the pedestals of sculptures has been used as waterbasins. Over the years, the stone waterbasin has often taken on a purely decorative role and is now used in every type of garden.

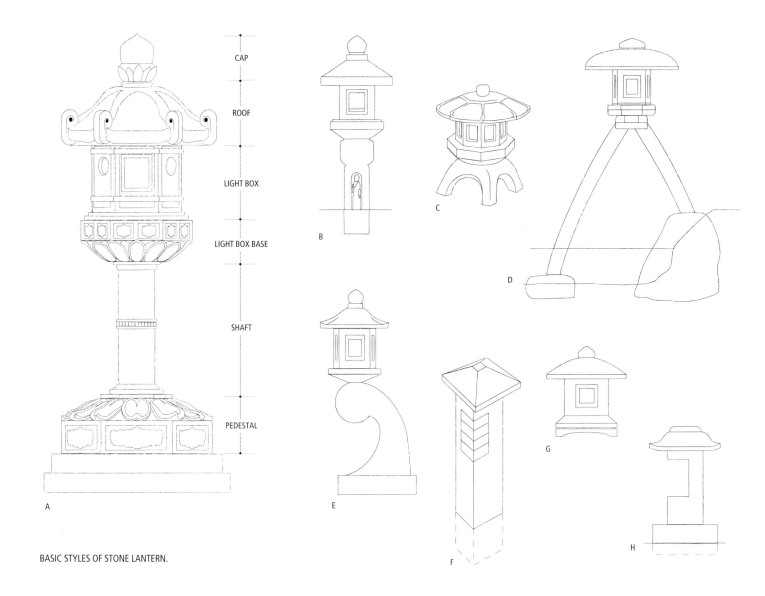

CAP

ROOF

LIGHT BOX

LIGHT BOX BASE

SHAFT

PEDESTAL

A

B

C

D

E

F

G

H

BASIC STYLES OF STONE LANTERN.

STONE LANTERNS

Stone lanterns (*ishidoro*) have a very long history, and the oldest existing lantern at Taimaji in Nara Prefecture is believed to date from the eighth century. Probably first imported from Korea at that time, they were used for lighting the grounds of Buddhist temples and later at Shinto shrines. They were also given to temples as offerings, and even to this day some temples boast rows and rows of hundreds of stone lanterns. Although they are generally about 1 1/2 to 2 yards in height, a great variety of sizes is found among the numerous types. In the sixteenth century, the stone lantern was incorporated into the tea ceremony garden and from there to gardens in general. A large number of forms evolved, which were named after the place they were first found (usually temples and shrines), the names of the person accredited with their creation, their shape, or their original use. Some lanterns are quite rustic in appearance, often being made of natural stones piled one on top of another to approximate the shape of a lantern, with some provision made for a light box. In general, a weathered appearance is favored, and while granite is the preferred material, softer stone is often used simply because it weathers more quickly. Basic shapes consist of the six-part *tachigata* type (of which the *Kasuga* lantern is the most common), with a pedestal, round shaft, light box base, a light box with four to eight sides, a roof, and an onion-shaped cap; the *Oribe* type, with the shaft planted directly in the ground; the *yukimi* type, with a broad roof, no shaft, and from three to six legs; the Valley lantern; the Signpost type; and a "placed" type (*okigata*), which is similar to a hand-carried lantern. The following list details these basic types:

STONE LANTERN VARIATIONS.

Top row, left to right: A large rustic lantern (*yamatoro* style) made of blue stone. Stone lantern at Kosenji temple in Kyoto paired with round, stone tsukubai. A stone lantern at Katsura Villa.

Bottom row, left to right: A square type of the usually round *Nuresagi* lantern. *Komachi-* style lantern. Oribe-style lantern.

Kasuga Lantern (A)

Named for Kasuga Shrine in Nara, this is one of the oldest lantern styles dating at least to the Heian period (794–1185). It is distinguished by a hexagonal light box with upturned corners, a round shaft, and richly detailed decoration.

Oribe Lantern (B)

Named for the tea master Furuta Oribe who succeeded Sen no Rikyu. Though it is unclear whether Oribe actually designed this lantern, it seems certain that it was designed specifically with the smaller, simpler tea garden in mind. Its distinctive feature is a squared-off shaft, which is partially buried in the ground and often carries an image of a bodhisattva, Christian saint, or some other figure on the visible section of the shaft.

Yukimi Lantern (C, D)

This so-called snow-viewing lantern is most often used to reflect light off a pond surface. Its chief character- istics include a large, low roof and a short profile, with the light box and pedestal mounted on between three and six legs. One distinct variation of this type is the *Kotoji* lantern, which usually has two long, curved legs, one of which is set directly in a pond so that the light box is over the pond surface.

Valley Lantern (E)

This lantern, called *rankeigata* in Japanese, is similar to the *Kotoji* in that its light box is directly above the

Sasaki Yoji uses a strip of lighting inside a channel to penetrate the entrance of his Osaka home. Passing under the wood-lattice doorway by Sakamoto Akira, it creates a "trail of fire" which deconstructs the confinement of space into interior and exterior.

pond surface. However, it has only one leg, which curves up and over the pond. A *Kasuga*-type light box sits atop the leg. It is highly ornamental in appearance.

Signpost Lantern (F)

So named because it was ostensibly used to light signposts (*michi-shirube*) at road junctions (or perhaps because it looks like a signpost itself). Often found in gardens today probably because of its "modern" appearance, the signpost lantern consists of nothing more than a square post planted directly in the ground with one corner cut for the light box.

Okidoro Lantern (G)

Rather than a single lantern, this is a class of lantern that is generally the smallest of all types. Consisting of one to three parts, it is very simple and rustic in appearance and usually used where illumination is needed close to the ground or where it can be easily placed on a ledge or stand, almost like a hand-carried lantern.

Sleeve Lantern (H)

The distinctive feature of this lantern (*sode-gata*) is that it has no light box of its own but is intended as a covered stand on which a hand-carried lantern is placed.

LIGHTING

Lighting in the Japanese garden was traditionally achieved by placing oil lamps in the light box of a stone lantern and by placing portable lanterns where required. The limited availability of light before the advent

Garden designer Ogino Toshiya uses simple lighting fixtures, shielding them from direct view here and there with tall grasses, in this simple *kare sansui* garden in Ashiya, Hyogo Prefecture.

of electricity meant that light needed to be focused on the task at hand, which is why the stone lantern and the waterbasin are so closely associated. Other typical locations for outdoor lighting were along footpaths, bridges, and near the pond surface. Today, stone lanterns mostly play a decorative role, but lighting in the garden has expanded to include accent lighting under trees, underwater lighting, and lighting anywhere a utilitarian or dramatic use can be imagined. In other words, it is now inconceivable to think of the garden without electric lights. Therefore, considering potential areas for lighting is essential in your garden design.

Utilitarian Lighting

Safety and security are two prime purposes of outdoor lighting. Safety means that paths, steps, bridges, gates, and the water's edge are all candidates for lighting. Generally, this would be limited to lighting focused downward and spreading from a source located close to the ground. Security lighting would include entrances and exits and might be temporarily activated by motion sensors. These lights would generally be wide-angle spots mounted on a wall or post. Dark corners where a person could hide unseen would also be ideal for such lighting.

Dramatic Lighting

Dramatic lighting in the garden can take the form of accent lighting under large trees, strings of miniature lights hung on trees, spotlights focused on various features, underwater lighting, and strips of light-emitting diodes (LEDs). However, advances in lighting technology can be a double-edged sword, leading to both greater flexibility and excess. To avoid excessive lighting, the guiding principles of naturalness and a search for essential beauty should inform your lighting choices just as they guide the design of the overall garden. As a general rule, avoid highlighting the "interesting shapes" of the lighting equipment itself. A low level of light, reflected on leaves and water, is enough to enhance the night views of your garden.

LIGHTING IN A SMALL VERANDA GARDEN
by Yagi Kenichi

I've chosen to illustrate some outdoor lighting techniques in the context of a veranda garden. A small veranda, such as our approximately 1 1/2-by-2 1/2-yard example, is the only space available to millions of apartment dwellers wishing to bring nature a little closer to home. Some unique problems present themselves when creating a veranda garden. Let's look at several of these problems and some creative solutions first.

- In many cases, permanent modifications cannot be made to the apartment by the renter, or must be approved by a management committee in the case of cooperatives. For these reasons easily removable modifications—such as the gravel and compressed-clay floor surface and suspended, cedar-plank wall in our example—can be employed.
- Weight limitations require creative solutions such as using building insulation-foam to change floor levels or create mounds over which pebbles or soil and grass can be successfully layered. Our example uses 2-inch-thick (5-cm) foam over which the same thickness of pebbles and clay is added. This produces a 4-inch-thick (10-cm) floor surface with the weight of only 2 inches (5 cm).

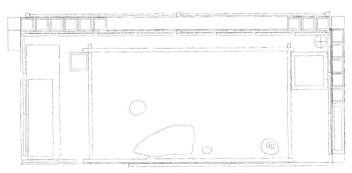

VERANDA LAYOUT.

WALL FRAME AND FLOOR.

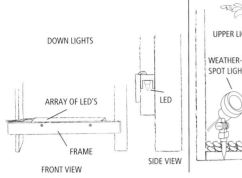

DOWN LIGHTS

ARRAY OF LED'S

FRAME

FRONT VIEW

DETAIL, PATTERN 1.

LED

SIDE VIEW

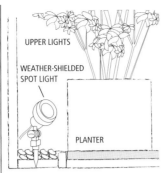

UPPER LIGHTS

WEATHER-SHIELDED
SPOT LIGHT

PLANTER

LIGHTING PATTERN 1

This example shows two popular types of indirect and atmospheric lighting: downward lighting emanating from behind the wood-plank wall, and upward-facing lighting under plantings. Two weather-shielded spotlights of 50 watts each were used for uppers, and two strips of LEDs were used as down lights. LEDs are available in full- or low-voltage types. Low-voltage lighting requires a step-down transformer but can be safer and easier to install than full-voltage lights. The uppers are a weather-shielded exterior type attached to a mounting pole. The pole is stuck down through the pebbles and into the foam to hold it in place and the angle of the light is adjusted. The down lights are exterior type LEDs of 2 to 3 watts each, arrayed in strips of varying groups of 18 lights, 36 lights, and so on, attached to the frame behind the cedar boards. The wires are carried around to the left side, concealed behind the boards, and connected to a transformer (in the case of low-voltage lights) or plugged directly into an exterior outlet.

LIGHTING PATTERN 2.

LIGHTING PATTERN 2

Perhaps the easiest and most atmospheric choice is setting candles at various points around the veranda. Here they are set in flower-shaped stands in various positions and heights. One type of candle-stand commonly seen in Japanese gardens simply involves cutting a length of bamboo (3 to 4 inches/7 to 10 cm in diameter) at a sharp angle from just above a joint. Place a candle inside the bamboo and stick the bamboo into the ground (or foam in our case), deep enough to stabilize it. The steep angle of the cut serves to protect the flame from wind and acts as a reflector. While candlelight can be successful in many situations, safety considerations limit the use of candles to places where no young children or pets are present and to windless, rainless days—although covered oil lamps may be an alternative at these times. In addition, consider the use of paper or glass diffusers to reduce the shadows and glare caused by exposed candle flames.

Along with the candles, I have added a solar-powered, outdoor lamp that is equipped with a motion sensor and timer which allows its 10 watt halogen light to turn on whenever there is movement, turning off after a fixed period of time. Wall-mounted solar spotlights are also available.

LIGHTING PATTERN 3

This example uses two adjustable, fixed spotlights of a medium-wide beam (40 to 60°), attached directly to the wall above the door frame. The light base is affixed to the wall, with the wire running inside the wall and connecting directly to the existing wiring (perhaps best left to an electrician), or along the outside of the wall to an exterior outlet and switch. A full-voltage or low-voltage light can be used. Low-voltage lights (12 volts, 24 volts, and others) usually require a step-down transformer (consult your lighting supplier for the appropriate type). This arrangement provides strong and even light but it can make a small garden look a little flat. To enhance the three-dimensional feeling, a single low-wattage spotlight (about 40 watts) can be used in combination with the lighting in pattern 1. Another alternative in the case of this veranda is to direct the spots upward to reflect off the overhanging ceiling, softening the overall light. A third possibility is to use three or four spotlights of very narrow focus (10 to 20°) to highlight areas like the leaves of the gardenia and the stones set into the clay, creating greater variation between lit and unlit areas.

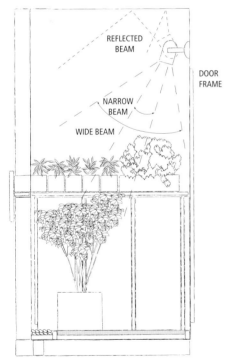

REFLECTED
BEAM

DOOR
FRAME

NARROW
BEAM

WIDE BEAM

DETAIL, PATTERN 3.

YAGI KENICHI is an architect and registered landscape architect. He worked with Kisho Kurakawa for over seven years before founding his own office. His work is primarily large-scale, landscape design for public parks and housing developments. He periodically lectures at a number of universities in Japan and is the author of a book on landscape design for beginners.

—"When setting about to design a garden, amateurs and professionals alike tend to think in terms of a sunlit, afternoon image. But unlike artificial, indoor environments, the natural environment is subject to constant changes, not the least of which is the light itself. Within a single day, you have full-light, sunsets, and darkened skies, all of which create any number of changing garden views. And each of these will vary with the season. Because light has no form in and of itself, it is somewhat difficult to visualize. In the past, it was common to use black or dark blue paper and draw with white to simulate various lighting conditions. These days, computer simulations have made visualizing various lighting conditions easier and more accurate for professionals. But anyone can experiment with lighting by setting lamps or flashlights behind or above various objects to simulate the actual situation before drawing up a plan."

CHAPTER 5

PLANTINGS AND OTHER GARDEN FEATURES

This *kare sansui* garden runs the length of a totally open artist's studio in Tondabayashi, Osaka Prefecture. The photograph shows the view that is revealed to the visitor as he reaches the top of a small set of stairs to the entrance gate. The finished garden is a powerful and sensitive statement that reflects gardener Ogino Toshiya's keen attention to the physical and emotional character embodied in individual trees.

Plum Estate Kameido by early nineteenth-century *ukiyo-e* artist Hiroshige Ando exaggerates the distance to the picnickers by forcing the viewer to look through the dark form of the plum tree.

Sasaki Yoji, professor at Kyoto University of Art and Design, relates how he was inspired to become a landscape architect by a photograph of the work of Mexican architect Luis Barragan. True to this original ideal, he creates a masterful courtyard garden, where natural and manmade materials engage in an ever-changing interplay of light, shadow, and color on a stage of white gravel and pristine white walls. Even the planting of the Japanese maple at a precipitous angle seems to animate a dialog between stone and tree, as intimate as that between a loving parent and a child.

In this chapter we will look at some aspects of planting and maintenance that make a Japanese garden unique, as well as stepping stones, walkways and other features that are closely associated with gardens.

When we think of plantings, several aspects immediately distinguish the Japanese garden visually from its Western counterparts. In order to achieve the overall harmony and tranquility that we have sought to achieve so far, planting must take into account three basic points: the color, shape, and size of plants and trees.

Color in the Japanese garden is primarily green. Flowers—other than those of flowering trees and shrubs—are noticeably absent. The range of plantings is intentionally limited, with materials and layout carefully combined to reflect aspects of the natural habitat and to highlight changes of season. One aspect of the color of plantings relates to the discussion of creating a background, middle ground, and foreground discussed in Chapter 2.

For example, dark green, broadleaf evergreens planted at the far side of the garden create a solid dark background all year round. Standing in front of that, a layer of paler and somewhat shorter evergreen and deciduous trees creates a visually lighter middle ground. To further emphasize depth, flowering deciduous trees like plum, with white or light-pink blossoms, are placed in the foreground. Smaller shrubs with deep red blossoms can be strategically placed to guide the eye back into space.

The shape that plantings take depends on whether they are naturally or artificially cultivated. In other words, all trees and shrubs are maintained by pruning and trimming for the purpose of keeping them healthy or to prevent them from growing past the desired size. The distinction is that some trees are also pruned to clarify, enhance, and clean up the natural form, while other trees and shrubs are artificially shaped to enhance ornamental or functional qualities, for example, as a natural barrier.

The overall appearance of the garden depends to a great degree on the size of trees and shrubs. Especially when starting with young plants, their eventual size needs to be anticipated. But given the potential for plants to exceed your anticipation, trimming for size as well as shape is essential to maintain the intended design.

Size is also related to color in terms of volume. For example, in the above discussion of dark evergreens planted as a background to the garden, it is the large volume of continuous dark color that creates the desired effect. If the dark trees are too fine or interspersed with lighter colors of equal amounts, the distance effect of the dark trees would be lost. On the other hand, a single dark form strategically located in the foreground, such as the wide, dark trunk of a mature plum tree, creates a visual "pressure" that the eye

One of Japan's most interesting architects, Take-hara Yoshiji strongly believes in the house as a place that supports the interactivity of a community—a community called "the family"—that lives within it. A single structure is more like a group of buildings and gardens where occupants find themselves unconsciously moving between indoor and outdoor space as they pass from room to room.

is forced to look past, enhancing the visual depth of the garden. This device was often seen in the prints of *ukiyo-e* masters such as Hiroshige.

In considering a planting scheme remember that plants thrive in their natural habitat. The plants discussed here are all available in numerous varieties (camellias alone number in the hundreds), many of which will suit the natural habitat where you live. In choosing the proper varieties for your garden, consider soil conditions, average high and low temperatures, sunlight or shade, rainfall, and maintenance needs. Draw up a rough layout with the general types you have in mind, then consult your local nursery on the most appropriate varieties for conditions in your area.

PREFERRED PLANTINGS

The Color Palette and Traditional Plantings

With some exceptions, where more dramatic color is introduced, the palette tends toward reds, purples, pinks, and white, rather than yellows, blues, or oranges (with the exception of autumn leaves). Particularly favored as flowering trees and bushes are the cherry (*sakura*, the blossoming of which is a major social occasion and the reason for much revelry in Japan), apricot or plum (*ume*), magnolia (*mokuren* or *kobushi*), and camellia (*tsubaki*). All these produce white, pink, or red blossoms, depending on the variety. With many flowering trees, for example, the cherry and apricot, the blossoms depart within a few weeks, spraying the ground with color as they leave.

Other Trees and Shrubs

While not within this limited palette, sweet osmanthus (*kinmokusei*) is a flowering, treelike shrub often found in the garden. Its tiny yellowish orange flowers herald the arrival of fall with a sweet, intoxicating scent before they scatter on the ground, forming a ring of gold around the trunk.

The Japanese maple (*momiji*), while neither flowering nor within this palette, is the very image of autumn in Japan, cherished for its delicate foliage and autumn colors of flaming red, yellow, and orange.

Often associated with water, the weeping willow (*yanagi*) is another deciduous tree favored in the garden, together with a number of fruit trees, including the Japanese persimmon (*kaki*), which yields a large, edible, orange fruit between late autumn and early winter. A single *kaki* fruit, hanging from an otherwise barren branch, is a favorite motif in Japanese art.

Bamboo (*take*), though technically a grass, can grow over 20 yards tall. More common in gardens are varieties that reach no more than 2 to 3 yards. Bamboo is an attractive plant, especially in small stands, due to its bright green stalks that grow straight and tall within a very limited space. In hot and wet climates, some varieties grow almost too fast, spreading their roots over great distances and sending up new shoots where they are not wanted. So choose a variety of bamboo that can be easily contained. Bamboo is not suited to cold or dry climates.

Left: A small forest of tall bamboo at Kenkoji temple in Yokohama. *Right*: Haircup moss (*sugigoke*) is a beautiful and delicate ground cover that doesn't take well to traffic, one reason it is often found nestled between protective stepping stones.

Azaleas (*tsutsuji*) are by far the most common flowering shrubs in Japan. They are almost always pruned into hedges or rounded shapes, which are sometimes interspersed with stones. The shrubs may be placed independently or linked to others and shaped to suggest waves or mountain ranges. One of the most extreme examples of shaping is the Japanese garden of Daichiji temple in Shiga Prefecture (near Kyoto), where the hedge twists and coils in an almost sculptural fashion through the garden.

Wisteria (*fuji*) is a vine that is often found twisted, trellised, and trussed in such a way that it comes to resemble a tree with an enormous canopy. Its abundance of fragrant, purplish-pink clusters of flowers hanging below leaves of bright green is a sensual delight.

While deciduous trees and perennials are enjoyed for their seasonal changes as well as for their beauty, evergreens are an equally essential element in the Japanese habitat, especially broadleaf evergreens. These are ubiquitous in the Japanese garden and are the main reason that Japanese gardens can maintain their greenness all year round. Natural broadleaf evergreen forests in Japan extend from the southernmost islands to a latitude north of Tokyo. Evergreen oaks, camellias, laurels, aucuba, and box are just some of the trees and shrubs in this group.

Evergreen trees of the coniferous variety often seen in gardens include numerous varieties of pine (*matsu*, especially black, red, and white pine), cedar (*sugi*), juniper (*ibuki*), Japanese yew (*ichii*), and others. However, given a choice of only one tree to plant in the garden, most people would probably choose the symbol of the Japanese garden—the pine—particularly the gnarled Japanese black pine. The meticulously shaped pine found in gardens today may have lost some of its significance as an evocation of the seashore, but the cultivation and care of the trees, whether black, red, or white pine, continues to be a worthy and satisfying pursuit for many.

The shaping and maintenance of the Japanese pine is an arduous and long-term labor of love. Most people usually leave the task to trained gardeners who go from house to house, while trees for new gardens are often purchased already trained from nurseries. However, the basic principle of shaping is not difficult to grasp and easily mastered by the weekend gardener.

Typically, the trunk of the tree is forced into a vertical zigzag by angling it and tying it to stakes from the time it is about 1 1/2 yards tall. Left and right branches are removed alternately to emphasize the curve of the trunk. The remaining branches are tied to bamboo poles to train them to grow more horizontally than their normal growth pattern, and any downward-facing branches are cut off. With mature trees, large rocks are sometimes tied to a thick branch to pull it down to the desired angle. New buds are plucked to reduce the number of new branches and help sustain the growth of existing ones. Finally, old and downward-facing needles are picked off by hand or clipped until all the tufts point upward. The aim is to create a sort of "hyper nature" by paring down and enhancing the characteristics of the tree, evoking the image of a weathered tree on a windswept rocky seashore.

Grasses and Moss

Lawns (*shiba*) are not used in traditional Japanese gardens, although they have appeared, particularly in stroll gardens, at least since the Edo period (1600–1868) and are common today. The favored variety of grass is a thickly matted, fine-leaf type such as zoysia Japonica or Korean grass (*korai*) that does not require frequent cutting. This grass spreads and grows well just about anywhere except heavily shaded areas or where water accumulates. In winter it becomes dormant, turning a beautiful golden brown, like a thick carpet of dried straw.

Architect Yokouchi Toshihito mixes a deep green groundcover with the lighter green of ferns and a Japanese maple in this elegant courtyard design. The scenery will change drastically when the leaves of the maple turn orange and red and yet again when they fall—creating a riot of color in the form of a contrasting red-on-green carpet.

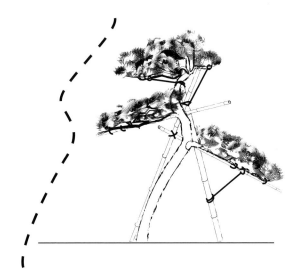

SHAPING A PINE TREE.

BEFORE PRUNING

AFTER PRUNING

COMPOSITE OF PRUNING POSSIBILITIES.
A. Suckers. **B.** Low growth. **C.** Excess, crowded branches. **D.** Dead branches. **E.** Vertical growth. **F.** Crossing branches. **G.** Downward growth. **H.** Growth extending beyond the silhouette of the tree.

Throughout Japanese history, Kyoto has been the center of garden theory and development, and this partly accounts for the popularity of moss in the Japanese garden. Kyoto is situated in a basin that receives abundant rainfall and is hot and humid in the summer months. Its soil naturally retains some moisture while allowing quick drainage, a condition that makes it perfect for growing most varieties of moss (*koke*). Moss gets most of its moisture from the air, so humid conditions with low levels of light serve it best. The large number of varieties, its soft and lush green appearance, and its intricate growth pattern also make moss a popular choice. Varieties such as hair cup moss (*sugi-goke*) that are common in the Kyoto area require constant care to grow in dry or cold climates. In such climates, varieties such as Irish moss, or a substitute ground cover such as sweet woodruff (which also produces tiny white flowers), baby's tears, or even herbs such as parsley and thyme might work better.

Long-blade grasses and bamboo grass are used in any number of places, such as between rocks; around the bases of fences, lanterns and waterbasins; and as natural boarders to demarcate areas not to be walked on. Ferns (*shida*) and flowering perennials such as irises (*shobu*) are used in wet areas around waterfalls, streams, and the shallow areas of ponds, especially where a marshy or mountain stream effect is desired.

PRUNING AND SHAPING

As mentioned at the beginning of this chapter, pruning is aimed first of all at keeping the tree healthy. Old branches, dead branches, and "suckers" growing from the base of the trunk are the first candidates for removal by pruning. Next, thinning out some of the denser growth allows sunlight and air to circulate and reach the interior branches and leaves. Where rain is frequent, larger trees may require thinning in order to let the heavily shaded ground under the tree dry out. While light pruning can be performed any time, heavy pruning is seasonal. With deciduous trees, pruning is carried out in late autumn after the leaves have fallen. With broadleaf or coniferous evergreens, major pruning is undertaken in the spring or early summer.

Aside from these requirements, pruning in the Japanese garden is carried out with an eye toward enhancing the shape of the tree—what I previously referred to as "natural" cultivation. This type of pruning involves removing unsightly branches—such as those growing out past the ideal silhouette of the tree, as well as inward-turning and crisscrossing branches—and encouraging branch growth in excessively bare areas of the tree.

Artificial cultivation involves pruning and cutting to create shapes not normally found in nature, either for the purpose of creating ornamental trees or to maintain the overall harmony of the garden. The latter most commonly takes the form of clipping shrubs into rounded shapes, which may be found singly or in groups, often in combination with stones.

Both squared and rounded hedge trimming are found in Japanese gardens, generally as a natural fence surrounding the exterior of the garden, or to line paths or walkways leading to the entrance, usually on the outside of the garden. Within the garden proper, shrubs joined to create elongated mounds are often used to echo distant mountains or rolling hills, as a way of visually uniting the garden with the surrounding scenery (see Chapter 2).

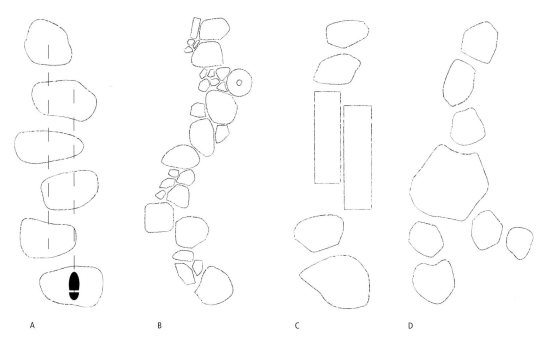

A   B   C   D

STEPPING STONES AND WALKWAYS

From their simple beginnings in the Zen-inspired space of the tea garden around the end of the sixteenth century, stepping stones (*tobi ishi*) and walkways of stone (*nobedan*) became an increasingly formal element of the design of Japanese gardens with the advent of the stroll garden in the early Edo period. Some of the finest examples of stepping stones and walkways are found at the imperial Katsura Villa in Kyoto. This villa incorporates a number of teahouses and gardens, linked together by walkways in a beautifully landscaped environment.

The primary difference between stepping stones and walkways is that stepping stones are placed one by one, with an interval between them that relates to a comfortable walking stride. They allow the passage of only one person at a time. Smaller stones do not invite stopping for long and are often only large enough to place one foot on comfortably, much like the step in a staircase. Larger stones serve specific functions: to indicate where one should pause to take in the view, as a junction for diverging paths (*fumiwake ishi*), or to provide an interface between home and garden for the removal of shoes. When a surer underfoot surface is needed, or one wide enough for more than one person to walk side by side, stones are grouped together to produce a walkway. The variety of combinations and shapes created for stone walkways is almost as vast as that of individual stones created by nature. In deciding which will best serve your needs, you will need to consider the advantages of each.

Here are some basic principles to consider in the layout of stepping stones:

1. As with other types of stonework, a part of the stone is buried in the ground or cemented in place. In the case of stepping stones, a height of 1 to 4 inches (2 to 10 cm) above ground is typical. The actual height depends on the scale of the garden, the size of the stones, and other factors, not least of which are safety and personal taste. Natural, rectangular-shaped, and round stones are used.
2. Key points to be observed in the layout of stepping stones are the overall "meandering" of the pathway, the right-left relationship between adjoining stones, and the shape of junctions where paths converge. Space between stones should be more or less even and determined by a normal walking stride.
3. Sometimes stepping stones are placed to allow passage across a stream or a pond. In this case, the stones are a little wider and very tall—anywhere from 2 to 3 feet under water (60 to 90 cm), plus at least a foot (30 cm) above the water line. Processed stone is often used to insure that the top surface is flat. The stones must be carefully spaced and leveled to insure safety.
4. A path through a garden generally begins at the garden side of the house, where a rather large stone with a flat top is placed. This is called a "shoe-removal" stone (*kutsunugi ishi*) and also serves as a place to put sandals used for walking in the garden. When an elevated deck has been built between the house and the garden, this stone serves as a step up to the deck. This stone is a formal element of the garden and should be included even where the level of the garden and the interior floor are virtually

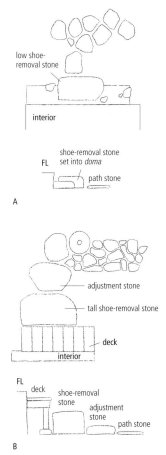

A long entryway mimics the outer and inner tea garden within this traditional Kyoto-style home by architect Kawaguchi Michimasa. Large stepping stones set in compacted clay lead past a gallery and studio to an inner entrance hall and courtyard garden (*tsubo niwa*).

An unusual stone walkway by Oguchi Motomi zigzags its way across this *kare sansui* of dark-gray gravel.

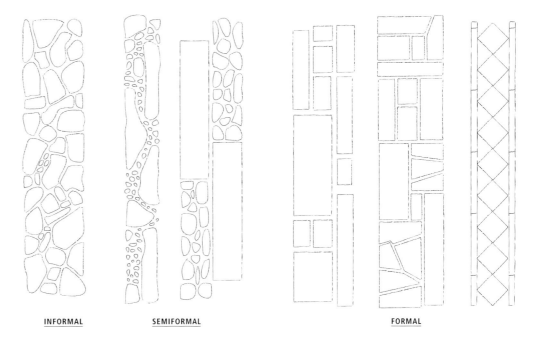

INFORMAL SEMIFORMAL FORMAL

PATTERNS OF STONE WALKWAYS.

the same, whether you remove your shoes before entering the house or not. In such a case the stone is set to be only slightly higher than the stepping stones that will come after it.

5. With a high deck or interior floor level, one or two companion stones are often used with the shoe-removal stone to create a smooth transition to the higher elevation. In tea gardens, the shoe-removal stone is usually taller and smaller than that used for the house, and another stone may be positioned to the right as a place to put a handbag or a fan momentarily.

Here are some additional tenets to consider when building a walkway:

1. Generally speaking, walkways are elongated sections of stone grouped in a rectangular shape. Stones are set so they are the same height and are grouped close together so the gaps between them are narrow or filled with mortar. In other words, the overall effect is one of a single unit, and walking on it is similar to walking on a cobblestone pavement.

2. The guiding principle behind the layout of walkways is called *shin, gyo, so*, referring to arrangements considered formal, semiformal, and informal. The words apply both to the arrangement of stone walkways and their individual elements (and to garden design and architecture as well). For example, a strictly square or round stone is considered formal (*shin*) as opposed to a rough, natural shape that can be considered informal (*so*). In terms of arrangement, a strict geometric pattern of straight-sided stones is considered formal, whereas a combination of straight-sided and natural shapes is considered semiformal (*gyo*). In terms of use, a more formal walkway—especially one with square-cut stone and greater width—might be used at the main entrance to the house or an entrance used by elderly people who require a sure footing. On the other hand, a walkway consisting of a lot of smaller, natural stones might be ideal for the entrance to a tea garden, where a rural or casual feeling is appropriate.

3. Because the stones are greater in number and placed closer together than stepping stones, smaller stones can be used, but all the stones must be cemented in place. "Belt stones" (*obi ishi*) and "label stones" (*tanzaku ishi*) are long, cut slabs that are, respectively, narrow and wide, and are used in walkway groupings (although label stones are also employed individually or in pairs, often in layouts with stepping stones).

■ ■ ■

Before ending this chapter with instructions on building a stone walkway, it may be appropriate to "step back" and look at the entire picture. When deciding which plants, features, or structures to include in the garden, remember that the garden we are aiming for is a simple and uncluttered environment, not an amalgamation of interesting parts. Don't try to do too much or feel pressured about getting it perfect. Aim for a comfortable learning process and a relaxing, pleasant outcome. A garden evolves over time. Watching the changes from season to season, even as you influence their direction, will afford many hours of quiet reflection and simple joy.

BUILDING A WALKWAY IN THE SEMIFORMAL STYLE
by Oguchi Motomi

Here I will introduce the basic steps for creating a stone walkway (*nobedan*) in the semiformal (*gyo*) style. The finished path should be easy to walk on and beautiful to look at. This walkway runs parallel to the building. The one pictured in the finished garden runs perpendicular to the entrance.

OGUCHI MOTOMI lives in Nagano Prefecture, north of Tokyo, where he has been designing gardens for thirty years. He has created well over three hundred gardens, most of them in private homes, as well as larger gardens in Korea, Austria, and Taiwan. He is also the author of eighteen books on garden design and history, and a practitioner of the tea ceremony (*chanoyu*) and of Japanese flower arrangement (*ikebana*).

—— "*In the middle of the busy city, hemmed in by neighboring houses and intruded upon by the sounds of urban life, we need a quiet space. It is my hope that the special character of the Japanese garden will assist you in creating a separate, peaceful world of your own. The approach to this creation is like that of the painter to his canvas. Unlike a park, this is a picture devoid of intrusions from the workaday world. At its best, it is a spiritual world, commanding an attitude of reverence just like any holy place. To achieve such a garden is to ask from its creator the highest level of philosophy, spirituality, and sensitivity. From this attitude, the finest efforts and best results are sure to flow.*"

DECIDE POSITION AND MAKE FRAME.

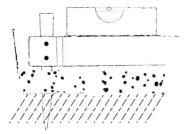

THE FRAME

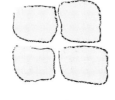

SET THE STONE

FILL THE FRAME AND CHECK THE HEIGHT OF THE STONE.

POOR ARRANGEMENTS

CHECK THE DEPTH OF THE SPACE BETWEEN THE STONE.

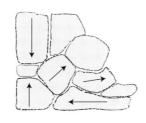

GOOD ARRANGEMENT

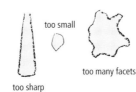

too small

too many facets

too sharp

POOR SHAPES

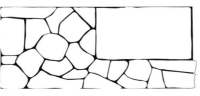

GOOD PROPORTION AND PLACEMENT

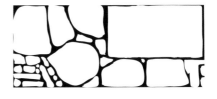

POOR PROPORTION AND PLACEMENT

1. Decide on the width, length, and position of the walkway by taking into account the size and theme of your garden, as well as its relationship to nearby elements such as stepping stones, the size of the entrances, and other materials you will be using. Choose a size and style that harmonizes rather than conflicts with other elements in the garden. (For example, if your garden is informal, don't use a formal-style walkway.)

2. Mark the shape on the ground in some fashion and dig out the area to a depth of 8 to 12 inches (20 to 30 cm) for stone that is 4 to 6 inches (10 to 15 cm) thick. Compact the earth with a hand or mechanical rammer.

3. Add sand or a rather dry mortar mix to about half the depth of the hole. In order to ensure that the outer border is straight, use a frame of wooden boards about 1 by 4 inches (2.5 by 10 cm). Hammer stakes into the ground outside the corners to hold the frame in place. Check the level of the frame and adjust as needed. Arrange your stones inside the frame, starting from one edge, with an eye toward a balanced, random mix of rectangular and rough stones. First make a trial layout on the ground next to your frame. The use of a frame is a valuable aid for first-timers, but with experience, or on very long walkways, string pulled tight around stakes and leveled can be substituted for a wooden frame.

4. In order to choose the best stones for the space, you should have two to three times the amount needed on hand. Generally, any stone will do so long as the top surface is flat. The size, number, and placement of the rough and square-cut stones, as well as their texture and color, will determine the overall feeling of the walkway. Use a wooden mallet to set the stone firmly in the mortar. Use a piece of two-by-four laid across the frame to ensure that no stones stick up above the others nor sink too far below. The stone should ultimately sit 3/4 to 1 1/4 inches (2 to 3 cm) above the final level of the ground.

5. When arranging the stone, be careful to avoid clear patterns or geometric shapes. When selecting or shaping stone, avoid specimens that are too sharp or fragile. Also avoid stones as small or as round as pebbles. When using large, squared stones, be sure to leave enough space next to the square stone for more than one natural stone. Keep in mind the relationship of the size of the individual stones to the overall size of the walkway.

6. Finally, check that the spaces between the stones are filled to a depth of about 3/4 of an inch (2 cm) from the surface of the stone. If not, add more mortar or sand. Spray everything lightly with water to clean the stones and set the mortar.

LIST OF PLANTS

Plantings in the following list are typical of those found in Japanese gardens. The list is by no means complete but broad enough to provide a selection suitable to any Japanese garden theme, style, or location. In addition, some conditions affecting planting are highlighted in the notes, with those conditions particularly affecting the Japanese garden marked with the letter J.

EVERGREEN TREES

ENGLISH	JAPANESE	LATIN	HEIGHT (MAX)	CONIFER	FLOWER / FRUIT	FRAGRANCE	SHAPE	SOIL / ENVIRONMENT
Birdlime holly, kurogane holly	kurogane mochi	Ilex rotunda	100 ft/30 m	no	small white flower/red berry	no	elliptical/pyramid	all/sun-shade
Black pine, Japanese	kuromatsu	Pinus thunbergii	100 ft/30 m	no	cone	no	pyramid	all/ocean side
Camphor	kusunoki	Cinnamomum camphora	50 ft/15 m	no	white flower	cut	round	all/ temperate
Chinese juniper	ibuki	Juniperus chinensis	65 ft/20 m	yes	cone	no	elliptical	temperate
Chinquapin	sudajii (shiinoki)	Castonopsis cuspidata	100 ft/30 m	no	acorn	yes	round	all/ temperate
Chusan palm, windmill palm	shuro	Trachycarpus fortunei	40 ft/12 m	no	yellow flower/fruit	no	fan-shape leaf	all/ warm-cold
Cypress, Japanese	hinoki	Chamaecyparis obtusa	130 ft/40 m	yes	cone	cut	pyramid	all
Daphniphyllum	yuzuriha	Daphniphyllum macropodum	33 ft/10 m	no	flower	no	pyramid	all/ temperate
Evergreen oak, Japanese	arakashi	Quercus glauca	30 ft/9 m	no	acorn	no	pyramid/round	all
Fir, Japanese	momi	Abies firma	100 ft/30 m	yes	cone	no	pyramid	moist
Hemlock	tsuga	Tsuga seiboldii	100 ft/30 m	yes	cone	no	pyramid	well drained/rainy
Loquat	biwa	Eriobotrya japonica	20 ft/6 m	no	yellow flower/fruit	yes	round	well drained/warm
Luster leaf holly	tarayo	Ilex latifolia	30 ft/9 m	no	red berry	no	pyramid	all/sun-shade
Red cedar, Japanese	sugi	Cryptomeria japonica	75 ft/23 m	yes	cone	cut	elliptical/pyramid	all
Red pine, Japanese	akamatsu	Pinus densiflora	65 ft/20 m	yes	cone	no	fan	all/dry
Sweet osmanthus, sweet olive	(kinmokusei)	Osmanthus fragrans (aurantiacus)	25 ft/8 m	no	yellow-orange	yes	elliptical	all/temperate
Tea camellia	mokkoku	Ternstroemia gymnanthera	50 ft/15 m	no	white/red berry	no	pyramid	warm/sunny
White oak (or bamboo oak), Japanese	shirakashi	Quercus myrsinifolia	65 ft/20 m	no	acorn	no	Pyramid/round	all
White pine, Japanese	goyo-matsu, hime ko-matsu	Pinus parviflora	65 ft/20 m	yes	cone	no	pyramid	all/mountain
Yew, Japanese	ichii	Cuspidata	30 ft/9 m	yes	yellow flower/red berry	no	pyramid	all/warm-cold

EVERGREEN SHRUBS

ENGLISH	JAPANESE	LATIN	HEIGHT (MAX)	CONIFER	FLOWER / FRUIT	FRAGRANCE	SHAPE	SOIL / ENVIRONMENT
Andromeda, Japanese	asebi	Pieris japonica	10 ft/3 m	no	white	no	round	acid/shady
Aralia, Japanese	yatsude	Fatsia japonica	8 ft/2.5 m	no	white flower/black berry	no	round	shade
Aucuba, Japanese	aoki	Aucuba japonica	6 ft/1.8 m	no	variegated leaf/red berry	no	round	well drained/shade
Azalea	satsuki	Rhododendron eriocarpum	6.5 ft/2 m	no	pink/red/purple	no	round	acid/well drained
Big sepal azalea	mochi tsutsuji	Rhod. macrosepalum	10 ft/3 m	no	pink flower	yes	round	acid/sun-shade
Camellia, Japanese	yabutusbaki	Camellia japonica	15 ft/4.6 m	no	red/pink	no	round/pyramid	well drained/sunny
Cape Jasmine gardenia	kuchinashi	Gardenia jasminoides	10 ft/3 m	no	white	yes	round	warm
Little leaf boxwood	tsuge	Buxus microphylla	8 ft/2.5 m	no	no	no	round	all/sun-shade
Nandin	nanten	Nandina domestica	10 ft/3 m	no	white/red berry/autum leaf	no	round	all
Photinia, Japanese	kanamemochi	Photinia glabra	30 ft/10 m	no	white/red leaf at first	no	round/elliptical	all
Podocarp	inu maki	Podocarpus macrophyllus	20 ft/6 m	no	red/blue fruit	no	elliptical/pyramid	all/warm
Sasanqua camellia	sazanka	Camellia sasanqua	20 ft/6 m	no	white/pink/red	no	round	well drained/sunny
Snow camelia, Japanese	yukitsubaki	Cam. Jap. Var. decumbens	13 ft/4 m	no	pale pink	no	round	well drained/sunny
Spear plant (Christmas berry)	manryou	Ardisia crenata	2 ft/60 cm	no	white /red berry	no	round	shade
Sweet daphne	jinchoge	Daphne odora	4 ft/1.2 m	no	white/purple	yes	round	neutral/well drained
Tea	chanoki	Camellia sinensis	15 ft/5 m	no	white	no	round	well drained/sunny

DECIDUOUS TREES

ENGLISH	JAPANESE	LATIN	HEIGHT (MAX)	SEASON	FOLIAGE / FRUIT / FLOWER	FRAGRANCE	SHAPE	SOIL / ENVIRONMENT
Apricot (or plum), Japanese	ume	Prunus mume	26 ft/8 m	spring	white/pink/rose flower/ green fruit	no	fan	moist/sunny
Babylon, Chinese weeping willow	shidare yanagi	Salix babylonica	35 ft/10.5 m	spring	no	no	round/droop	wet/ sunny
Chestnut, Japanese	kuri	Castanea crenata	65 ft/20 m	summer/fall	nut	yes	fan	all
Crape myrtle	sarusuberi	Lagerstroemia indica	25 ft/8 m	summer	white/pink/rose flower	no	fan	all/warm
Empress tree	kiri	Paulownia tomentosa	50 ft/15 m	spring	pale violet flower/fruit	yes	fan	all
Katsura tree	katsura	Cercidiphyllum japonicum	100 ft/30 m	fall	small red flower	no	fan	all
Magnolia	kobushi	Magnolia kobus	65 ft/20 m	spring	white flower	yes	fan	acid/warm
Magnolia (or tulip magnolia), Japanese	mokuren	Magnolia liliflora	12 ft/3.6 m	spring	violet flower	yes	fan	acid/warm
Maidenhair, ginkgo tree	icho	Ginkgo biloba	75 ft/23 m	fall	bean/bright yellow foliage	no	fan/elliptical	all

ENGLISH	JAPANESE	LATIN	HEIGHT (MAX)	SEASON	FOLIAGE/FRUIT/FLOWER	FRAGRANCE	SHAPE	SOIL/ENVIRONMENT
Maple, Japanese	momiji (iroha kaede)	Acer palmatum	30 ft/10 m	fall	red/orange/Fr/Fl	no	fan	all
Mountain cherry, Japanese	yama zakura	Prunus donarium var. spontanea	80 ft/25 m	spring	white flower	no	fan	all/sunny
Persimmon, Japanese	kaki (ama)(shib)	Diospyros kaki	60 ft/18 m	fall	orange fruit (round) (oblong)	no	fan	all
Pomegranate	zakuro	Punicia granatum	20 ft/6 m	summer	orange/red fruit	no	fan	all/ sunny
Snowbell (Styrax), Japanese	egonoki	Styrax japonicus	65 ft/20 m	spring/summer	white	yes	fan	All/moist
Weeping cherry	shidare zakura	Prunus cerasifera pendula	65 ft/20 m	spring	whitish pink flower/Fr	no	fan/droop	all/sunny
Yoshino cherry	somei yoshino	Prunus x yedoensis	30 ft/9 m	spring	pale pink flower/Fr	no	fan	all/sunny
Zelkova, keyaki	keyaki	Zelkova serrata	65 ft/20 m	fall	bronze-red leaf	no	fan	all

DECIDUOUS SHRUBS

ENGLISH	JAPANESE	LATIN	HEIGHT (MAX)	SEASON	FOLIAGE/FRUIT/FLOWER	FRAGRANCE	SHAPE	SOIL/ENVIRONMENT
Althea	mukuge	Hibiscus syriacus	10 ft/3 m	summer–autumn	lavender/white/pink flower	no	elliptical/round	all/sunny
Azalea (Temate-leaf Azalea), Japanese	mitsuba tsutsuji	Rhod. dilatatum	6.5 ft/2 m	spring	reddish purple flower	no	round	acid/shade
Bridal wreath (Thunberg spiraea)	yukiyanagi	Spiraea prunifolia	8 ft/2.5 m	spring	white flower	no	fan/drooping	all/sunny
Bush clover	miyagino hagi	Lespedeza thunbergii	5 ft/1.5 m	sum/fall	reddish purple flower	no	round/drooping	all/shade
Bush clover	yamahagi	Lespedeza bicolor	6.5 ft/2 m	sum/fall	reddish purple flower	no	round	all/shade
Hydrangea	ajisai	Hydrangea (species)	5 ft/1.5 m	summer	blue/purple/pink flower	no	round	moist/shade/acid
Quince, Japanese	kusa boke	Chaenomeles japonica	10 ft/3 m	spring	red-orange flower/ yellow fruit	no	fan/round	all
Saxifrage (Deutzia)	utsugi	Deutzia crenata	10 ft/3 m	spring	white flower	no	round	all
Spice bush, Japanese	kuromoji	Lindera umbellata	10 ft/3 m	spring/fall	yellow/green flower/ black berry	cut	"spindle" round	all
Tree peony	botan	Paeonia suffruticosa	7 ft/2.1 m	spring–summer	red, white etc. flower	yes	round	all/sunny
Wisteria, Japanese	fuji	Wisteria floribunda	100 ft/30 m (vine)	spring	violet flower, 20-in clusters	yes	climber	all/sunny

HERBACEOUS PLANTS, PERENNIALS, GROUND COVERS, ETC.

ENGLISH	JAPANESE	LATIN	HEIGHT (MAX)	SEASON	FOLIAGE/FRUIT/FLOWER	FRAGRANCE	SHAPE	SOIL/ENVIRONMENT
Balloon, bell flower	kikyo	Platycodon grandiflorum	3.3 ft/1 m	summer–fall	violet/white flower	no	round	sunny/all
Bamboo (many types)	take (general name)	Phyllostachys species	65 ft/20 m	—	—	no	straight stalk	wet/warm
Cast iron plant	haran	Aspidistra elatior	2 ft/60 cm	—	evergreen	no	clump	moist/shade
Chrysanthemum	kiku, kogiku, etc.	Chrysanthemum species	3.3 ft/1 m	fall	various	no	single-triple stem	all/sunny
Dwarf bamboo	sasa	Sasa spp.	6.5 ft/2 m	—	—	no	clump	dry-wet/hot
Fern (ex: American maiden-hair)	shida (general name)	Filicopsida adiantum (pedatum)	1.5 ft/40 cm	—	—	no	clump	wet/shady
Field grass	shiba, koraishiba	Zoysia japonica	2 in/5 cm	—	brown/gold	no	creeper	sunny
Fringe pink	nadeshiko	Dianthus superbus	2 ft/60 cm	summer–fall	pink/white/rose flower	yes	clump	all
Hair cup moss	sugigoke	Polytrichum juniperi	4 in/10 cm	—	evergreen	no	moss	moist-well drained
Hardy terrestrial orchid	ebine	Calathe discolor	1.7 ft/50 cm	spring	pale brown/white/yellow flower	no	clump	sunny
Hollyhock, wild ginger	tachi aoi	Asarum species	1 ft/30 cm	spring	red/purple/white flower	no	round	all
Iris, Japanese	hana shobu	Iris ensata	2 ft/60 cm	summer	violet/yellow/white flower	no	round	wet/sun-shade
Iris (rabbit-ear iris), Japanese	kakitsubata	Iris laevigata	2 ft/60 cm	summer	violet/white flower	no	single stem	wet/sunny
Lotus	hasu	Nelumbo nucifera	1.7 ft/50 cm from pond surface	summer	white-pink flower/large leaf	yes	—	pond
Maiden grass (Eulalia)	susuki	Miscanthus sinensis	5 ft/1.5 m	fall	whitish tuft	no	clump	well drained/sunny
Morning glory	asagao	Pharbitis nil	vine	summer	blue, white, pink, etc flower	no	climber/drooping	all
Orchid (hyacinth)	shiran	Bletilla striata	2.1 ft/70 cm	spring	red-purple flower	no	clump	wet/shade
Stonecrop	taitogome	Sedum (oryzifolium)	6 in/15 cm	spring	very small yellow flower/ evergreen	no	mosslike	well drained/sunny
Water lily	suiren	Nymphaea	sits on pond surface	summer	white-pink flower/large leaf	yes	—	pond

NOTES

TREE NAMES: Latin is always the most reliable name when ordering a plant for the garden. English and Japanese names will vary.

HEIGHT: A maximum height has been listed for general guidance. However, height often varies according to country, weather, soil, and many other factors.

SEASON: Depending on location, climate, and other local conditions, the flowering season or fall leaves may vary. Check with your local supplier for more accurate dates.

FRUIT AND FRAGRANCE: Two choices that greatly affect planning strategy and maintenance are the use of fruit-bearing trees, such as Japanese persimmon, and fragrant trees, such as sweet osmanthus (sweet olive). Though initially one might fall in love with a particular scent, tastes can change over time. Then, too, people have widely varying reactions to scent and unlike falling leaves that can be swept away before the neighbor complains, a strong scent cannot be "cleaned up." Fruit trees may seem like a great idea at first, but keep in mind that a large tree will yield a couple of bushels of fruit which need to be picked and disposed of every year. In other words, a nice feature can quickly turn into a burden.

A related consideration is the differences between dual- and single-gender plants. Where separate male and female plants exist, differences can be substantial. For example, the female ginkgo tree yields a popular bean-like fruit that is roasted and eaten but, in its raw form, has a very bad odor. For this reason male plants are usually preferred.

SOIL QUALITY AND ENVIRONMENT: These are general conditions that can be mediated somewhat by planting strategy (i.e., shading trees that should not get too much sun) or choice of species (i.e., using more sun-tolerant or water-tolerant plants). Soil quality will affect not only the health of the plant but its ultimate size, ability to flower, and even flower color (e.g., higher acidity can lead to a bluer flower in some plants).

WET AND DRY CONDITIONS: Japan is a country of generally heavy rainfall and high humidity. Most of the plants in this list, therefore, will do well in such conditions. The mainland of Japan, other than Hokkaido, is in a temperate zone similar to a stretch from Georgia to New York. Cold, dry air blows southeast from China and Russia in the winter and hot, moist air, northeast from the South Pacific in the summer. In addition, Japan has a monsoon season that brings heavy rains through June and July, and a typhoon season that brings rain and strong, gusting winds in September. The southerly areas (not including Okinawa) from Kyushu through Shikoku and about half of Honshu see little to no snow while northern Honshu and Hokkaido are snowed in four to five months of the year. Therefore not all plants can be used in all climates, but enough of a variety is listed here to satisfy most situations.

YEAR-ROUND GREENERY VS. SEASONAL COLOR (J): The Japanese garden, it has been previously noted, favors broadleaf evergreens, with deciduous trees such as the maple or cherry to highlight seasonal changes. Obviously, in specific usages such as hedges, evergreens are a practical as well as aesthetic consideration. However, even in such cases, choosing flowering shrubs can add seasonal color.

MAINTENANCE REQUIREMENTS AND COSTS (J): A concern for any garden, but particularly for a Japanese garden, is maintenance. Well-trained pines, for example, require regular pruning to keep their shape, and ponds with koi need care to keep the fish healthy and the water unsoiled. In Japan, small house gardens are often cared for by professional gardeners who typically make the rounds in the spring and fall. Doing it yourself helps to mitigate costs. Raking sand, mending bamboo fences, repairing clay walls, or resetting stepping stones are all a part of Japanese garden maintenance.

INITIAL COST VS. INITIAL IMPACT (J): Simply speaking, fully-grown trees are expensive but give immediate effect as opposed to waiting five years or more to have younger trees come into their own. Yet younger trees are easier to transplant and adapt to a new environment more readily. Building a tea house, for example, may put limitations on your planting budget but planting a beautiful tea garden makes little sense until the tea house is in place. In other words, "big ticket" items are probably best done first while plantings can be added gradually one at a time.

ACKNOWLEDGEMENTS

I would like to thank Yagi Ken for getting my feet on the right path and keeping them there and for kindly appearing in this book. Also for generously giving of their time, instruction, and photographs, Oguchi Motomi, Masuno Shunmyo, and Yasumoro Sadao. These four gentlemen are the pillars on which this book was built.

I would also like to thank Professor Suzuki Makoto for allowing me access to his original research on *kare sansui*, and all the fine architects and garden professionals who gave of their work and experience to help make this book worthy of publishing.

Finally, my personal thanks to Barry Lancet and Michiko Uchiyama of Kodansha International for their confidence and support, and to my dear wife Naomi.

BIBLIOGRAPHY

Art of Setting Stones, The, Mark Peter Keene, Stonebridge Press, 2002.
Garden as Architecture, The, Toshiro Inaji, Pamela Virgilio, Kodansha International, 1990.
Gardens of Japan, The, Shigemori Mirei, Nissha Printing Co., 1949.
Gardens of Japan, The, Teji Itoh, Kodansha International, 1984.
Guide to the Gardens of Kyoto, A, Marc Treib, Ron Herman, Kodansha International, 2003.
Ikkyu and the Crazy Cloud Anthology, translation by Sonja Arntzen, University of Tokyo Press, 1986.
Inner Harmony of the Japanese House, The, Atsushi Ueda, Kodansha International, 1990.
Japanese Gardens, Design and Meaning, Mitchell Bring, Josse Wayembergh, McGraw-Hill, 1981.
Japanese-Style Gardens of the Pacific West Coast, Melba Levick, Kendall H. Brown, Rizzoli, 1999
Japanese Touch for Your Garden, A, Kiyoshi Seike, Masanobu Kudo, David Engel, Kodansha International, 1980.
Japanese Traditional Gardens, Yoshinobu Yoshinaga, Shokosha Publications, 1958.
Journal of Japanese Gardening, Douglas M. Roth, Roth Teien, bi-monthly.
Landscape Gardening in Japan, Josiah Conder, Kodansha International, 2002.
Magic of Trees and Stones, The, Katsuo Saito, Sadaji Wada, Richard L. Gage, Japan Publications Trading Co., 1964.
Makino's Illustrated Flora of Japan, Hakuryukan Co., Ltd., 2000.
Plants for American Landscapes, Neil G. Odenwald, Charles F. Fryling Jr., Thomas E. Pope, Louisiana State University Press, 1996.
Reading Zen in the Rocks, François Berthier and Graham Parkes, University of Chicago Press, 2000.
Secret Teachings in the Art of Japanese Gardens, David A. Slawson, Kodansha International, 1987.
Themes in the History of Japanese Garden Art, Wybe Kuitert, University of Hawaii Press, 2002.
Website, www.jgarden.org, Robert Cheetham.

PHOTO CREDITS

The publisher is grateful to interior magazine *Confort*, published by Kenchiku Shiryo Kenkyusha Co., Ltd., for permission to reproduce the photographs on page 53 (shot by Asakawa Satoshi) from Issue No. 50, 2001, and to Hermès Japon for permission to publish the photographs on pages 2-3 and 55 (shot by Sobajima Toshihiro).

Asakawa Satoshi   pages 1, 4–5, 10–11, 12–13, 15, 16, 21 (top), 22, 34 (8), 35, 36 (bottom), 41 (top right & left; bottom left) 49, 53 (courtesy of *Confort*, by Kenchiku Shiryo Kenkyusha), 61, 63, 64–65, 68, 69, 71 (bottom left), 74 (top), 75, 78, 83 (top)
Oguchi Motomi   pages 20, 30, 31, 34 (3, 5), 40, 44, 71 (top right & center; bottom right & center), 83 (bottom), 84 (top), 85
Tabata Minao   pages 47, 56–57, 59
Hirota Haruo   pages 27, 38, 52
Sugino Kei   pages 39, 72, 73, 76
Hata Ryo   pages 6–7, 26, 80

Takasaki Yasutaka   pages 34 (4), 42, 67
Kobayashi Koji   pages 8, 14, 18–19
Sobajima Toshihiro & Hermès Japon   pages 2–3, 55
Masuno Shunmyo   page 58
Maeda Makoto   page 23
Fukuzawa Akiyoshi   page 77 (top)
Miwa Akihisa   page 62
Kaneko Shigeru   page 50
Nobuhara Osamu   page 36 (top)
Tokyo National Museum   page 77 (bottom)
Joseph Cali   pages 17, 34 (1, 2, 6, 7, 9), 37, 41 (lower right), 45, 71 (top left), 74 (bottom), 79

CAPTIONS

page 1: Rough stone and a compacted-clay wall present a sober but surprisingly warm welcome in this apartment house and garden by Watanabe Akira. The stark strength of the entrance highlights the more delicate and ephemeral beauty of the garden that lies beyond.

pages 2–3: An installation by architect Kori Yumi at the Maison Hermés gallery in Ginza, Tokyo, as part of her ongoing exploration of "change" in the context of a search for that which is truly eternal. The changing light streaming through architect Renzo Piano's glass-block walls, captured by the raked gravel, becomes the subject of the work.

pages 4–5: The quiet and contemplative nature of the Zen garden is in part a result of enclosing the garden and framing the view, as seen in this delicate courtyard garden (*tsubo niwa*) by architect Nagasaka Dai.

pages 6–7: Architect Yokouchi Toshihito revisits the classic courtyard garden, emphasizing the amorphous flow between interior and exterior space, indicative of traditional Japanese housing, with an exceptionally deep and sunlit hallway (*engawa*).

ILLUSTRATIONS

All illustrations by the author, except those on pages 9 and 20–21.

新しい和の庭　THE NEW ZEN GARDEN

2004年5月14日　第1刷発行

著　者　ジョセフ・キャリ
発行者　畑野文夫
発行所　講談社インターナショナル株式会社
　　　　〒112-8652　東京都文京区音羽 1-17-14
　　　　電話　03-3944-6493（編集部）
　　　　　　　03-3944-6492（営業部・業務部）
　　　　ホームページ　www.kodansha-intl.co.jp
印刷・製本所　大日本印刷株式会社

落丁本、乱丁本は購入書店名を明記のうえ、講談社インターナショナル業務部宛にお送りください。送料小社負担にてお取替えいたします。なお、この本についてのお問い合わせは、編集部宛にお願いいたします。本書の無断複写（コピー）は著作権法上での例外を除き、禁じられています。

定価はカバーに表示してあります。

© ジョセフ・キャリ 2004
Printed in Japan
ISBN4-7700-2981-0